THE
WORLD *Mythology*
SERIES

Gods and Heroes
from
Viking Mythology

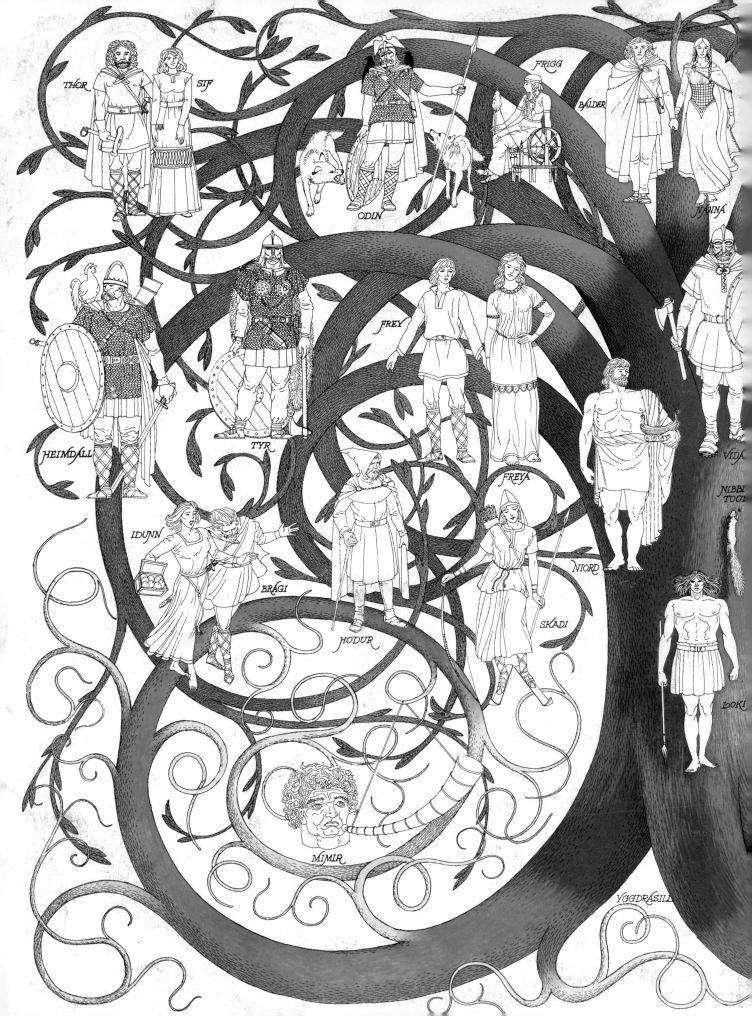

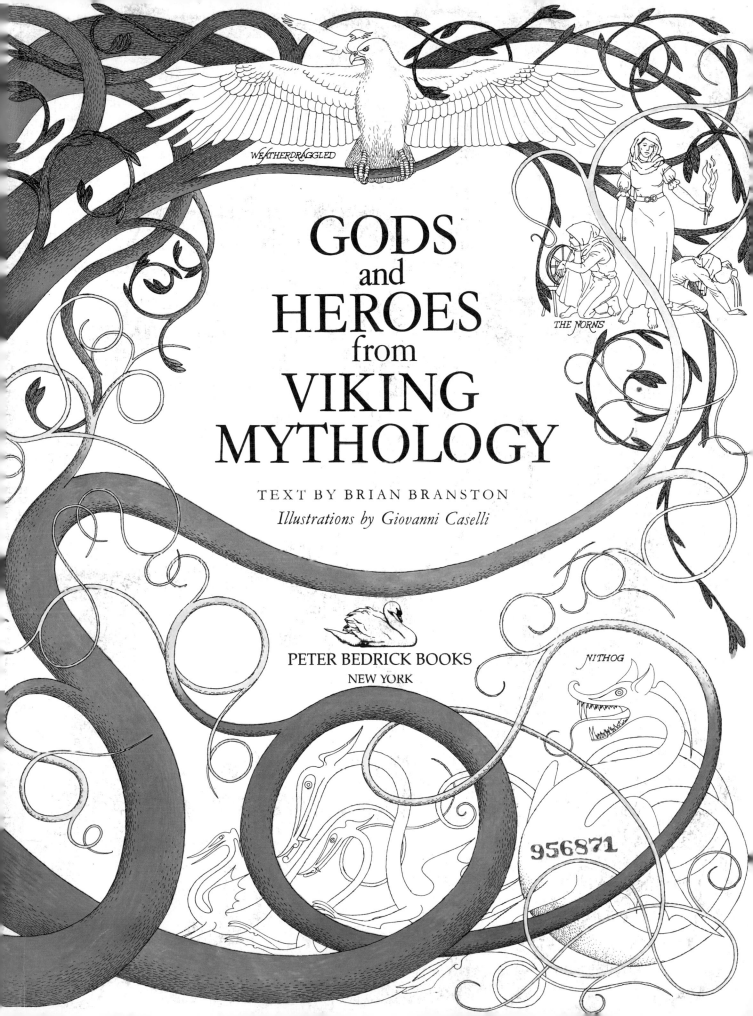

WEATHERDRAGGLED

THE NORNS

GODS
and
HEROES
from
VIKING
MYTHOLOGY

TEXT BY BRIAN BRANSTON

Illustrations by Giovanni Caselli

PETER BEDRICK BOOKS

NEW YORK

NITHOG

956871

Published by
Peter Bedrick Books
2112 Broadway
New York, NY 10023

Printed in Italy
5 4 3 2 1

This edition 1994

THE ARTIST
Giovanni Caselli is an Italian from Florence who, since
the early 1960s, has been involved in researching and
preparing reconstructions of life in the past.

Library of Congress Cataloging-in-Publication Data
Branston, Brian L.
  Gods & heroes from Viking mythology /
  text by Brian Branston; illustrations by Giovanni Caselli.
  (The World Mythology series)
  Originally published: London : P. Lowe, 1978
  Includes index.
  Summary: A collection of myths about Thor, Balder,
  King Gylfi, and other Nordic gods and goddesses.
  ISBN 0–87226–905–1   ISBN 0–87226–906–X (pbk.)
  1. Mythology, Norse—Juvenile literature.
[1. Mythology, Norse.] I. Caselli, Giovanni, 1939– ill. II. Title.
III. Title: Gods and heroes from Viking mythology. IV. Series.
[BL860.B66   1993]
229′.13–dc20   93—29705

THE AUTHOR
Brian Branston worked as a BBC producer and film
director and was for ten years head of the BBC's Travel
and Exploration Unit, taking an active part in some of
the adventures and films he was directing. He has filmed
in Iceland, Greenland, North and South America and off
the Great Barrier Reef. His published work includes
books on Anglo-Saxon and Scandinavian mythology.

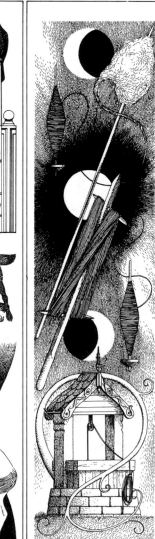

Contents

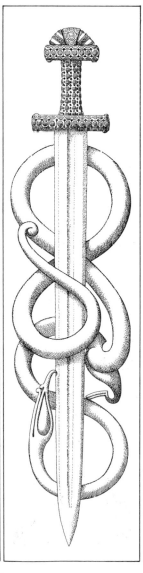

The tricking of King Gylfi

Long ago, in the old days, there ruled in Sweden a king called
Gylfi. King Gylfi loved his northland, even in the bitterly cold
winters when, for months on end, the sun never shone and
the gloomy forests and mountains were hardly illuminated by the
shadowy light reflected from snow and ice. Poor people then
were glad to keep close in their cabins, burning the logs they had
chopped in the autumn to see them through, while the famished
wolves flitted between the trees like ghosts and frequently
snuffled up to the barred and bolted doors.

But in spring and summer the sun returned from the south,
warming the pine-scented air, and the ice on the lakes and rivers
melted. Bears woke from their winter sleep, scratched their
heads and lumbered off through the woods searching for honey.
Birds sang for joy and every leaf and pool flickered with light.
At that season King Gylfi loved Sweden best of all and he had
no intention of losing a sod or pebble of it, which he might well
have done, for the times were unsettled and violent. Not only
were the kings of Sweden, Norway and Denmark frequently at
cross purposes and likely to attack each other, but bands of
filibustering Vikings, owing allegiance to nobody, plundered the
coasts of the north in their fearsome dragon longships.

King Gylfi was well prepared against these pirate fleets. His
warriors were garrisoned up and down the country in circular
strongholds with earth and stone walls mounded ten ells high and
with on top, a palisade of tree trunks taller than two men.
Inside these forts his henchmen and their families, and their
horses too, lived in thatched roofed barracks grouped in fours to
form a defensive square. King Gylfi was never in any fear of
an attack from foreign armies or Vikings, and every night in his
castle hall he slept the untroubled sleep of a man at peace with
the world and with himself. But he *was* destined to lose part of
his kingdom and in a very mysterious way. It all started with the
woman.

The woman who was to disturb King Gylfi's peaceful life was
unlike the women of the north. She was tall, certainly, but her
complexion instead of being fair was sunburned. Her eyes were

not blue but brown and her long hair, instead of being golden-white was black and in some lights almost purple. She looked more like the occasional slave-girl brought captive to the north by Vikings who had sailed far away to the great city which they called Micklegarth.

Those parts were dangerous and enchanted, peopled by dwarfs, giants, monsters and magicians. If she turned out to be a sorceress nobody need be surprised. And many – wise after the event – said they knew from the first that she was a witch, an enchantress who could cast powerful spells. Everybody had heard the Vikings' tales of the lands to the far south where the seas were hot and the burning deserts threw up spell-cast pictures luring thirsty men to their doom. It was clear that if you sailed any further south along that coast you would reach the threshold of the flame-guarded kingdom of Surt the fire giant. Few sailors had dared to venture that far and even fewer had returned to tell about what they had seen. There could be no doubt at all that if the woman came from there she was indeed an enchantress.

She had arrived at King Gylfi's town driving an ornately carved wagon with an embroidered awning. It was drawn by four oxen, but oxen bigger and stronger than any seen in the north before. Gylfi invited her to stay in his castle. Her shape and grace, her strange brown eyes, her dark hair which, when the torches on the walls were lit in the evening, shone with changing purple gleams and her scent of exotic ripe fruits and flowers fascinated the king. She cast her spell over him and within a few days he was willing to give her half his treasure. The woman said, 'No.' She wanted nothing. She was happy living in the north. But if King Gylfi really was insistent she would accept a place of her own to live, say an acre or two of his land.

The spellbound Gylfi had no hesitation in offering Gefiun (for this was her name) as much land as she could plough with her own four oxen in the space of a day and a night.

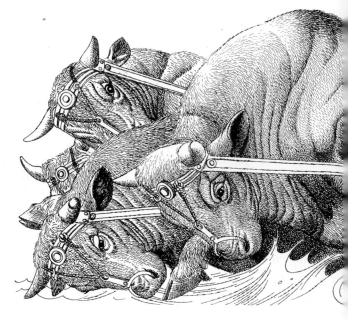

Where she got the plough from is still a mystery but people who saw her start her labouring in the mists of one early morning said the ploughshare appeared to be as big as a Viking ship. As for the four oxen, they were like hills moving, lumbering, straining and sweating and their eyes were burning lamps piercing the dim light of dawn. She started to plough before King Gylfi was out of bed, and by breakfast time the woman and her team had disappeared over the horizon.

All that day and that night also, neither she, nor her oxen, nor the plough returned to the castle. Gylfi went to bed. The woman had gone as mysteriously as she had come.

Next morning King Gylfi was awakened by a trembling of his bedroom walls accompanied by a distant rumbling. The heavy carved oak chairs began to hobble across the floor and his great bed, with him sitting up in it, slid towards the window. He hastily put his feet to the vibrating floorboards and pulled on his breeches. He staggered drunkenly to the battlements and for once could not believe his eyes.

The sun, which could only have risen five minutes before, was setting again! He shivered in the sudden darkness, but within another five minutes the sun was once more in the sky. King Gylfi pulled on his shirt, puzzling over this extraordinary happening: the sun doesn't rise twice on one day! But

even more extraordinary, the sun had set
sideways and had reappeared sideways like
the moon being obscured by a passing cloud.
Then he realized the staggering truth.
It was the land which was moving. He was
witnessing a new kind of earthquake and
before his startled eyes, as a line of
hills moved steadily towards the sea, the sun
appeared to bounce from one to the other
like a golden ball. All the time the noise of
grinding rocks, the clamour of frightened
birds and the splash and rattle of broken-off
rivers and streams was bewildering. He held
on tightly to the trembling stone balustrade.

King Gylfi thought he was still dreaming
until he saw, ahead of this colossal tract
of his kingdom, four giant oxen harnessed in
unbreakable traces hauling and heaving as
Gefiun urged them on. The countryfolk on
this massive moving land-island were still
trying to go about their daily lives. Gylfi
watched in astonishment as a shepherd boy
with his barking dog struggled to drive
his staggering flock through a gate which
wouldn't keep still; and a milkmaid in
a field kept falling off her stool and spilling
the milk.

What armies had failed to do, this
enchantress and her four giant oxen were
doing overnight: they were depriving Gylfi
of a vast region of his kingdom, they were
simply dragging it away.

Curiosity got the better of his astonishment.
He ran down to the courtyard and called
for his horse. When he had caught up with the
clouds of dust and been bogged to a halt
in the mud from the broken rivers, he was just
in time to see his stolen land being hauled
into the sea. Now the progress of the land
mass was easier and it left a wake in the
water behind it like that of a fleet of rowing
Viking ships. After a few miles its movement
stopped and the hills and fields settled down,
their roots firm on the sea-bed. Gefiun had
stolen part of Sweden and turned her booty
into a new island. In fact, to this day,
the island is called Sea-Land, or Zeeland. It is
now part of Denmark. The mighty chasm in
Sweden rapidly filled up with water to form
a lake which is now simply called Malaren,
the Lake.

King Gylfi was furious. He despatched
messengers to the stolen island and all over his
kingdom to search for the woman and
her oxen but they had disappeared off the face
of the earth. The oxen had returned to
Jotunheim, being Gefiun's own sons by a
giant; and Gefiun no doubt had gone back
to Asgard or its near neighbourhood, for she
turned out to be not from the south at all
but a relative of the old gods.

The people of the northlands called these
old gods the Æsir. They were ruled by Odin,
father of all the divine powers, whose home

was in Asgard. Nobody on earth knew exactly where Asgard was but most people believed it to be a land above the clouds. Gylfi's fury still smouldered against Gefiun and he determined somehow to seek redress. It seemed to him that the Æsir must be mighty magicians and he wondered if they made their own magic or were given power by other divinities whom they themselves worshipped. To find out, he started on a journey which he hoped would bring him to Asgard. King Gylfi himself was skilled in magic and he had no intention of being taken in by the gods a second time. So he altered his appearance, put on a pilgrim's tattered cloak and a dusty old slouch hat and, whenever anyone asked his name, said it was 'Wayweary'. There is no need to go into the years of wandering, the perils of his journey or the bitter disappointments King Gylfi encountered before he did at long last reach Asgard. He knew it was Asgard because of a splendid hall which he saw was roofed with war shields of pure gold. The guard before the great double-doors was whiling away the time by juggling with sharp pointed daggers and in fact had seven in the air at once.

Without taking his eyes off the flying daggers the man on guard said, 'Who are you, and what do you want?'

'I'm called Wayweary,' said King Gylfi, 'I've come a long way and, as you can guess from my dusty clothes and worn-out sandals, I'm very weary. Do you have a crust and a lodging for the night for a poor old tramp?'

The man caught his daggers one by one, looked suspiciously at Gylfi and said, 'As for lodging, you will need to enquire from the lord of the castle.'

'What is his name?' asked Gylfi.

'You will have to put that question to him yourself,' said the man and strode off inside the hall with Gylfi at his heels.

The interior of the hall was vast, indeed part of it appeared to be a battle-plain with a battle in full progress. The tumult and shouting were frightening. King Gylfi was forced every now and then to cringe,

expecting to be hit by a stray arrow or spear. He now knew exactly where he was, in Valhalla, home of the valiant dead, but the hurrying guard gave him no chance for further questions. The two turned away from the battlefield into a corridor which led to a high-raftered chamber, at the far end of which were three thrones with three personages seated on them. In the gloom it was difficult to make out what they looked like, but King Gylfi was filled with awe at their presence. His guide turned about and left him standing awkwardly. He broke the silence by asking, 'What may be your lordship's names?'

'High,' said one.

'Just-as-High,' said another.

'The Third,' said the last.

Knowing himself to be at last in Asgard and in the presence of the Æsir, King Gylfi felt embarrassed not to say apprehensive.

High said, 'What is your business?'

Gylfi replied, 'I am looking for someone who is very well-informed indeed; you might say the most well-informed being in earth or heaven. Is there anyone here of that nature?'

'You will be exceedingly fortunate to step away from here unharmed unless you are better informed than you appear to be now. What is it exactly that you want to know? Come forward and ask boldly,' commanded High.

King Gylfi said, 'Saving your worships' pardon I want to know who is the foremost and oldest of the gods, I want to know what he was doing before heaven and earth were created, I want to know where the frost giants and fire giants came from, who created mankind, the sun, moon and stars and why the winds blow . . .'

Just-as-High interrupted, 'It is obvious that you want to know the ins-and-outs of a lion's mouth and that's always a dangerous business.'

The Third said, 'You'd better draw up a stool, for the relating of all this is going to take a long time.'

And what King Gylfi found out you can now read for yourself.

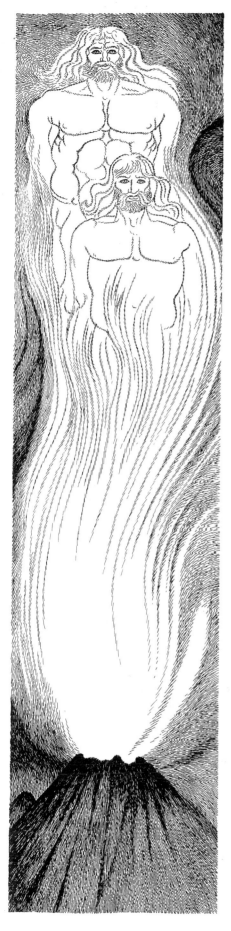

The world of ice and fire

In the beginning, the mysterious beings told King Gylfi, there
was Ginnungagap, the yawning void or the vast abyss. It was a
region so tremendous, so limitless that it extended for ever in
any direction, with space to contain a billion universes and still
find room for more. To contemplate it would make you sick with
dizziness, would make you weightless, would bend your mind
with terror for it had no length, no breadth, no up, no down. In
the beginning there was nothing in Ginnungagap that any
human thought could grasp, not a drop of water, a blade of grass
or a twig, not even a grain of sand. There was no light,
no darkness, no silence and yet no sound – only a yawning void.
Although this nothingness was so vast and shapeless, it was still
not empty. It had no form but it was definitely not empty.
Only the gods knew this secret. After the beginning, this nothing
began to be something and there were seen to be in it two
contrasting regions. First of all there was the region of fire, called
Muspellheim. No ordinary being could live there for the
land was ablaze and the air aflame. Later the combusting fire
giants were to make Muspellheim their home. Muspellheim means
'home of the destroyers of the world' and, as we shall
see before the story finishes, nothing could be more apt than this
terrifying name.

The Æsir took care not to approach the boundary of that
land for the heat was so intense, the flames so tremendous, that
even a million miles away they scorched and shrivelled
everything up. To make it even more frightening, Surt, the
fiercest of the fire giants, stood sentinel on the flaring borders
gripping in his flaming hand a sword of fire. He barred the way
to any intruder, including the Æsir, the gods. He was there at
the beginning and he would be there at the end, at the Ragnarok,
the doom of the gods. The hair of Surt was on fire, shooting
brilliant streamers in all directions like tethered comets; his
head and face were molten fire and streams of lava continuously
rolled down his mis-shapen body. No wonder it was
prophesied that at the end of the world he would fling singeing
flame and stinking smoke over all the universe and burn

everything that lived there to blackened ash!

The three strange informants told Gylfi that the second of the great regions in the vast abyss of Ginnungagap was a cold, bleak wilderness of ice and snow and freezing fog clouds, called Niflheim. Niflheim, like Muspellheim, had existed for countless ages before our earth was created. In the centre of Niflheim there surged and foamed up the mighty fountain of all waters, a raging gusher named Vergelmir, the Roaring Cauldron. All the rivers of all time proceeded from Vergelmir. Their names were fearsome and their forms were magic: Howling, one was called, others Storming, Frightful, Bubble-blasting. One was said to be composed entirely of chunks of ice fighting their way along in the shape of weapons – spears, javelins, swords and battle-axes.

Another tumultuous fountain in Niflheim was called Elivagar or Icy Waves. Elivagar, too, had welled up from its unknown source since time immemorial. Some say that Vergelmir and Elivagar were only different names for the one primeval fountain. However that may be, Elivagar's crunching, creaking, groaning mountains of ice expanded and exploded and spread layer upon layer as glaciers all over the whole of the northern quarter of Ginnungagap. And across the ever growing sierras of ice, whirled winds of hail, blizzards and frozen torrents of rain.

Most important, as we shall see, there bubbled up through Elivagar a poisonous scum which set like the slag which runs out of a furnace. This hardened into black ice. When the mass stopped and flowed no further it hung suspended, forming colossal icicles and icebergs log-jammed up and up, one on top of another. So between them, Vergelmir and the poisoned Elivagar completely filled the northern part of Ginnungagap. At last the yawning void which lay to the north quarter was blocked with heavy and crushing ice and frost; while in contrast, the southern sky of Ginnungagap glared with sparks and molten gases gushing out of Muspellheim.

It was quite obvious that after aeons of time the regions of fire and ice in the yawning void must meet. When this eventually happened there arose that most amazing of all phenomena, which no one since the world began has been able to explain – life. Where the two elements came together in space, the yawning void was as mild as the windless air, but as the ice of Niflheim touched the fire of Muspellheim there was a tremendous explosion and a mighty booming bang. The fermenting

drops of venom bubbling up through Elivagar were fused to life by the fire, and across the length and breadth of Ginnungagap there formed the body of a giant. He was shaped like a man and at first he hardly moved. A broth of bubbling and boiling mud and ice gave birth to his ferocious head, his arms, his torso and his sludge-streaked legs. His later descendants, the frost giants, named him Aurgelmir which means Mud Boiler, for they knew the secret of his creation; but others called him Ymir.

For long ages Ymir lay sleeping in his porridge of poisonous, seething mud and ice. At last his body was solid and he began to sweat. Under his armpit grew a male and female; then one of his feet mated with the other and produced a six-headed son. From these creatures sprang the race of frost giants.

Not all the ice of Niflheim was impregnated with the poison from Elivagar, and where it remained pure but was still melted by the fires of Muspellheim, a vast cow appeared in the thawing ice. Her belly spread across the heights as a colossal cumulus cloud and her legs were columns at the corners of space. From the udder of this great cow flowed four rivers of milk and on this milk the giant Ymir was suckled. The frost giants called her Authumla meaning the Great Nurse. Authumla herself needed sustenance and she

began to lick the continents of ice about her, finding them pleasantly salty to her taste. Just as a master sculptor sees in a block of marble an image which only he can release, so when Authumla licked the ice something new began to appear.

By evening of the first day her questing tongue had licked out the hair of a man. All next day she nuzzled and slobbered until a man's head appeared. By the third day she had licked a complete man into shape. The gods called him Buri for they claim him as their first ancestor: he was beautiful and bright to look at, a great and mighty god. As time went on, Buri had a son called Bor, a name which means 'born', for all those thousands of years ago there were still not very many words available. Bor's wife was Bestla the daughter of a giant known as Balethorn. Bor and Bestla had three sons called Odin, Vili and Ve.

All these beings, the ancestors of the giants and the gods, and the universal cow Authumla, had formed in the primeval formlessness of Ginnungagap. Because of the venom proceeding from Elivagar some were evil. Others, like Buri, were good. But it is well known that good and evil cannot live peaceably together and before long there was to be a tremendous battle between the cosmic powers.

The creation of the world

The frost giants were a dark and violent race, mis-shapen, monstrous and noisy. Old Ymir's son, born by the union of one foot with the other, was a glacier-like being with six heads called Thruthgelmir or Mighty Roarer, and *his* son was known as Bergelmir or Rock Roarer. When they and their ancient father and grandfather Ymir-Aurgelmir or Mud Boiler met in council the noise was ugly and Odin, Vili and Ve, the sons of Bor were irritated beyond endurance.

Odin and his two brothers quarrelled with the old giant Ymir and after a great battle they killed him. When he fell, hacked to pieces, so much blood flooded from his body that all his giant family were drowned except the youngest, Bergelmir, and his wife. Bergelmir swam through the billows of blood dragging his wife by the hair until he was able to scramble on to a giant mill and there they lay sprawled across the millstone gasping for breath. In this way, the race of the frost giants and hill ogres was able to continue.

Odin, Vili and Ve dragged Ymir's carcass, still pouring volumes of blood, into the middle of Ginnungagap. There were so many wounds in Ymir's body that the blood flowing out formed the sea. All oceans, lakes, rivers, waterfalls, pools and streams came from Ymir's blood.

The sons of Bor went to work on Ymir's body. They pounded, kneaded, chopped and slashed his tremendous corpse, pushing and pulling his flesh this way and that as though it were clay until they were satisfied. When they had finished the first part of their gruesome task they had produced the groundwork of the earth, rolling hills, plains, dry river beds, empty lakes, and the empty sea-bed. Into all these hollows they poured Ymir's blood so that the earth lay entirely surrounded by the sea with rivers running into it. His bones they hacked and splintered to make the mountain crags. They made individual rocks and seashore pebbles from his toes, double-teeth and remaining chips of broken bone. They used Ymir's hair for trees and bushes. From the soil made out of his flesh, the race of dwarfs appeared spontaneously rather like maggots. Bor's sons had now created the earth and the beaches and the sea but as yet there was no sky. So Odin, Vili, and Ve between them heaved up the mighty skull of Ymir to form a dome over the earth. Now they had to find a way to keep it in place.

Fortunately (because without a sky the earth would have been a dark and miserable, not to say uninteresting place to live in) a solution was at hand: they were able to make use of the dwarfs. Odin, Vili and Ve peremptorily ordered four of them to stand forever at the four corners of the world and to hold up the sky. They called them North, South, East and West. A little later on Odin created the winds by posting a giant (one of Bergelmir's sons) in the form of an eagle at the ends of the earth to flap his wings for ever. And into the stream of air Bor's sons cast Ymir's brains to make the clouds.

The dome of the sky was now firmly fixed, but it remained dark and menacing. Freed from supporting the sky, the sons of Bor caught the glowing cinders and sparks which are thrown up and blown up out of Muspellheim and poised them in the middle of the yawning gulf to give light to both heaven and earth. They appointed positions to all the stars: some were fixed in heaven, some were to pass backwards and forwards in regular patterns. In this way the seasons of the years were marked out, but as yet there was no sun and no moon, and day was not separated from night.

Odin, Vili and Ve now gave a great grant of land encircling the outward shores of the ocean for the race of giants to settle in, calling it Jotunheim or Giantland. Finally the young gods took Ymir's brows to build a circular stronghold of cliff-like walls around the earth. They called this fortress Midgard, the Middle Enclosure.

High, Just-as-High and the Third settled back on their thrones to see what effect their account had had on Wayweary, as King Gylfi still called himself. Gylfi was very astonished at the information he had received so far but, like most people, he was curious to know where the first man and woman, his own ancestors, had come from.

High said: 'You'll have to be patient. There is still information of a universal nature that we have to disclose. Don't you want to learn how day was divided from night, and how the sun and the moon were made? Or indeed what binds the universe together? You must remember that though men and women may be important to themselves, from the point of view of eternity they are very small indeed. Make yourself comfortable and listen.'

Night and day

We talk about things following one another as naturally as day follows night, but is it all that natural? We only think so because from the moment we are born until the moment we die, day *has* followed night. What would we do if night followed night and we never saw day again – or the other way around? We would soon be exhausted if we had no night in which to recuperate the strength we had used up during the day; and endless night is too frightening to think about. So it is obvious that a great deal of thought has gone into the ordering of the simple system where night and day follow one another.

This is how it all came about. Of course, the gods were at the bottom of it, but they turned to the giants to do the actual work. Narfi, one of the first giants to colonize Jotunheim, had a very beautiful daughter who was quite unlike the Viking women in appearance, having a dark complexion and dusky hair. Her name was Night. Beautiful as she was, she made herself more attractive by wearing bright stars in her long hair. Naturally enough, many men wished to marry her and being a young woman of strong character, she married three husbands, one after the other.

Night's first husband was a handsome young fellow called Naglfari or Darkling, who may well have been a distant cousin of hers. Their marriage did not last long, but long enough for them to have a son called Space. If you happen to be out alone on a dark night with no clouds and the stars twinkling away into infinity, you will be well aware of the presence of Space.

There was some mystery about Night's second husband. Nobody ever called him anything else but 'Another'. It looks suspiciously as if 'Another' was simply a bye-name, a name employed to disguise the person's real identity. People frequently speculated about who he could really be or where he came from. There seems no doubt that he was not a giant and if that was the case, then he must have been a god, for no other beings had been created at that time. It is probably too late now to find out whether Another was someone of supreme importance who felt embarrassed about acknowledging a relationship by marriage to the giants. Whoever he was, Night and her second husband Another had a lovely daughter who was named Earth. Now, here is the surprising thing: of all the gods, Odin himself also had a daughter called Earth – so people are left to draw their own conclusions.

Night's third and last husband was Delling, which means Dawn. He was definitely a relative of the gods and, as his name implies, he was bright and fair. Their son Day took after his father's side of the family and was very blond and beautiful.

It is clear that the gods knew all about Night and her various children and they were only too happy to work them into their scheme for the universe. The gods decided that each twenty-four hours should be divided into twelve and twelve and that half should be light and half dark. They gave Night and her son Day each a chariot and a pair of horses and sent them up to the heavens to drive around the earth, one after the other, once every twenty-four hours. Night drove first with her lead-horse known as Frostymane who each morning sprinkles the ground below with dew as he champs at his bit. The froth and glitter of his spittle can be seen as it gathers in beads on leaves and petals just before dawn. Behind gallops Day. His lead horse is called Shiningmane.

The resplendence of his two shining steeds and of his own long, golden hair, illumines all the earth and sky with light.
'Day and Night I can understand,' said Gylfi, 'but what about the sun and the moon? Are they the same, or were they created in a different way?'
'Ah,' answered High. 'That's another story.'

In the old days the sun and moon, made like the other stars and planets from the flames of Muspellheim, swung unguided across the heavens. At that time there lived on earth a man named Mundilfari. It is not clear whether he was of the giant race or a poor relation of the gods. His name means 'the world turner' and in the beginning he may well have been charged with making the world spin round – under the direction of the gods, of course. Perhaps this important work may explain his rather arrogant nature which, in the end, got him into trouble. It happened like this.

Mundilfari had two children so bright and handsome that he thought nothing in creation could compare with them except the sun and the moon. Proudly he called the boy Moon and the girl Sun. When the gods heard about this they took offence. Vainglory of this kind was too much for them to bear and they snatched the children away from their father and put them to work in the heavens.

They made the girl he had named Sun ride like a jockey on one of the horses pulling the chariot of the sun. They are a pair of fine, strong animals named Early-Wake and Supreme-in-Strength. Year after year, until the end of time, they follow their path across the sky, varying its height and length with the regular pattern of the changing seasons. Because the flaming heat of the sun would burn up any living thing that came too close to it, the gods fixed an indestructible shield known as Svalin or Iron-cool between the horses and the shining fiery chariot they draw, to protect both the animals and their driver from the blaze.

Sun's brother had to ride one of the horses of the moon but his journeys were much more complicated because the moon he was set to guide waxes and wanes each month so that it is never quite the same for two days together. Moon could not manage this by himself and he in his turn kidnapped two other children from earth. A little boy, Bil, and his sister, Yuki, had been sent up a high mountain by their father to fetch water from a well. That was the last the old man ever saw of them.

As Moon drove behind the peak in his glowing chariot, he snatched the unsuspecting children and took them along with him. On a clear night of the full moon they are still both visible: people on earth call them the children in the moon and it is they who make the moon wax and wane. How exactly they do this is a puzzle. No-one knows whether

they draw a curtain across the moon's face, or whether they perhaps persuade him gradually to turn his head sideways and then back again.

There is another story told about the heavens which has a more sinister significance. From the earth both the sun and the moon can be seen racing across the sky. This is not only because they are drawn by splendid, galloping horses. They have a pressing reason for losing no time in their journey: they are both being pursued by wolves.

A long, long way to the east of Midgard, where it is almost always winter and dark forests stretch as far as the eye can see, in one desolate ravine where the tree trunks are all corroded iron, live evil witches, troll-women known as Ironwooders. Evil breeds evil. The worst of these witches became the mother of dozens of giants, all born in the form of wolves. Their brutish father was himself a wolf or at least a werwolf and it is said that his name was Fenrir. Two of his cubs grew into such huge, terrifying animals that the powers of evil were able to set them like ravening dogs onto the sun and the ever-changing moon.

Bounding through the sky, the wolves chase the horses and the chariots as though they are rabbits or hares. One shaggy, dark wolf pursues the sun; the other, just as hideous, leaps along, following the moon. Sun and moon have no hiding place from these evil beasts and are doomed to run away until the end of time.

The prophecies say that in the end the wolves will overtake the sun and moon and swallow them up completely. The dome of the sky will be filled with blood as the sun's light is put out and fierce winds will scream around the darkened heavens. But that, of course, is in the far distant future and may not even happen.

'Well, that's a relief,' thought Gylfi to himself. 'But we still haven't found out how our first mother and father were made.'

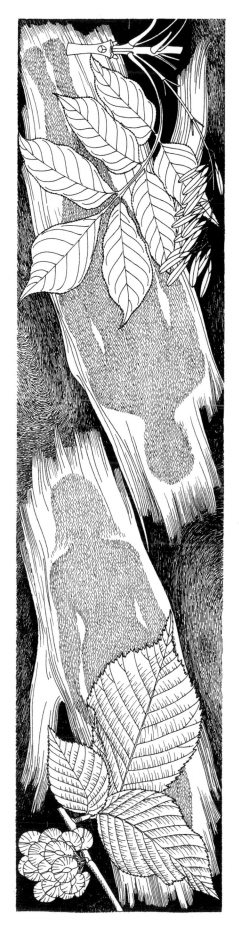

The first humans

The three sons of Bor were at first called Odin, Vili and Ve. While Odin always kept his name (except when he moved about the universe in disguise) Vili was sometimes called Hoenir and Ve was often known as Lothur.

One morning when all creation was new, the sons of Bor were walking together along the ocean shore. As they looked about them they could not help admiring the world they had made. The pure air sparkled with light for everything was running according to their plan – the sun was shining, the breezes were blowing enough to cool and refresh the skin, puffy white clouds adorned the blue sky and the waves splashed pleasantly along the vast, empty strand.

Empty? Well, not quite. In the distance, just beyond the waterline, the three gods made out two logs of driftwood. They had only recently been deposited on the yellow sand by the waves sweeping in from the ocean and were so near the water's edge that the ebbing tide still lapped the side of the one nearest the sea.

Odin looked at his brothers Hoenir and Lothur and a wild idea came into his head. Together they strode along the firm golden sand until they stood over the two logs. As the bay curved round, the sun happened to be behind them and Hoenir's shadow fell along the log nearest the water while Lothur's shadow lay along the other one.

Odin watched as the shadows of their legs and arms moved, making it look as if the logs, too, were moving. He dropped down onto his knees by the log nearest the shore; it had been the trunk of some primeval elm tree. Placing his lips to the rough bark he breathed out his divine spirit. Then he stood up and the three stepped back to watch.

Slowly the bark of the elm log began to shrivel and split and roll back until the body of a naked woman appeared. She was very beautiful but her skin was blanched like a plant grown for a long time without light and her eyes when they opened were vacant. She lay quite still without moving a limb.

Odin bent over the other log, which had come from an ash

tree. Once more he breathed on the thin bark and this time the figure of a man appeared in the wood. His eyes opened vacantly and he, too, lay motionless.

All this time the shadows of Hoenir and Lothur lay along the newly released bodies. The three young gods looked at each other and without speaking each knew what to do.

Odin had released Woman and Man and had given them a soul and life. Now the other two brothers made their gifts.
As Lothur looked down on the woman he transferred to her the flush of youth, the use of her five senses and the power of understanding. Slowly she sat up, looking around her in wonder at the beautiful world. Then she turned to look at the body still lying motionless and empty by her side.

Lothur then transferred his power to Man. The warmth of blood began to course through his veins and he, too, received understanding and the gifts of sight, hearing, smell, taste and touch.

Hoenir's gift was the faculty of speech.

The two new beings, the first man and the first woman, looked at each other in full understanding, rose to their feet and embraced. Odin called the man Ash and the woman Elm, from the trees out of which they had been formed. He took off his cloak and draped it over the woman and put his tunic round the man's shoulders. Together the first human beings turned away from the sea and walked hand in hand into their new world.

'Did the gods abandon them to their own devices after that?' asked Gylfi.

But it was clearly not yet time for this question to be answered: there was still much to tell about more important events.

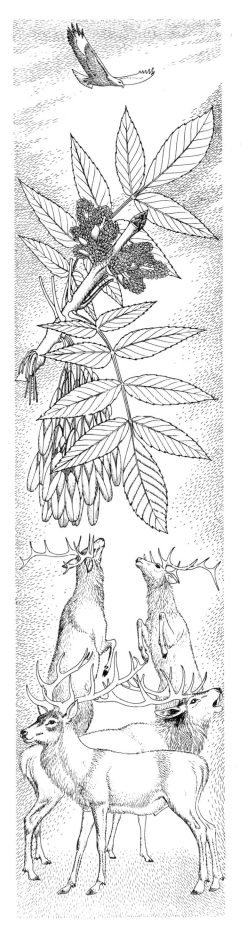

Yggdrasill, the World Ash

'It is no part of our intention to tell you where the World Ash Tree called Yggdrasill came from,' said King Gylfi's informants. 'That tree is simply *there*. You may not be able to see it from the earth, but take our word for it, it is there. Think of a force like that which exists between a magnet and a piece of iron. You know it is there although you can't see it or touch it. To mortals Yggdrasill may be invisible, but let me tell you, without the support of the great Ash Tree everything would disintegrate and explode into infinity.'

Yggdrasill is of all trees the largest and most stately. Its branches overhang all the nine worlds and spread out above the sky. There are three roots to the Tree, stretching far and wide to support its trunk and branches: one root reaches into Asgard where the gods live; the second winds out to Jotunheim where formerly the yawning void used to be; and the third twists down over Niflheim. These three roots are nourished by water from three wells. The well in Asgard is called after Wyrd, the most powerful of three sisters. These sisters are relatives of the moon and their influence over the destinies of men is limitless. There they crouch, wrapped in cloudy grey shawls, their faces hidden in the shadows of the folds. Their well is especially sacred, and they mix the water from it with the clay round its banks into a paste which they spread over the root. This counteracts the forces of evil and preserves the root for the liquid in their well is so holy that it turns anything coming into contact with it pure white and forms a skin like the protective film inside an eggshell. Their work prevents the limbs of the tree from withering or rotting. From heaven some of this purifying water descends as a sweet distillation onto the earth below. It is called honeydew by men, and bees are nourished on it. The well of Wyrd gives life to two white swans from whom all the swans that ever lived are descended.

Yggdrasill's second root burrows towards the frost giants. At its tip bubbles the well of Mimir. Once a god, only the head of Mimir now remains, kept alive by magic herbs. His head is full of wisdom because he drinks water from the well every day.

The head can still speak when it is addressed by the father of the gods, Odin. This is fortunate, for Mimir and his well hold the wisdom, the hindsight and the foresight of all eternity and at the end of time Odin must consult with Mimir if he hopes to save himself, the Æsir and his world.

Down below in Niflheim, the realm of mist and fog, is the third well, the bursting, boiling, violent Vergelmir. The third root of Yggdrasill hangs dark and slimy over the poisonous, foul vapour rising from Vergelmir's swelling waves. In that maelstrom wallows the winged dragon Nithog, the Dread Biter. His terrible jaws pierce the spray to gnaw at and injure Yggdrasill's root.

In fact, the things which continually harm Yggdrasill are almost too numerous to mention. Writhing with Nithog, squirming all through Vergelmir are broods of serpents which blow clouds of venom at the suffering root. Some of their names are Gnaw-Fang, Grave-Wolf and Root-Ripper. Then four gigantic stags strain up from their hind legs to browse on the leaves and tear the bark from the branches of the Tree, ripping away the foliage and covering without which it cannot live. In the topmost boughs of Yggdrasill perches a wise but peevish old eagle with a beak so big a hawk may sit on it. And a squirrel called Nibble-Tooth continually bounds from top to bottom of the Tree carrying abusive messages between the eagle and Nithog the dragon.

The story of how the Ash Tree got its name of Yggdrasill is a frightening one. Yggdrasill means 'the Steed of Ygg' and Ygg meaning 'Terrible One' is one of Odin's names. So Yggdrasill is literally 'Steed of the Terrible One'. Why should the Tree be Odin's horse? In the same way as the gallows-tree is sometimes called the hanged-man's horse. This is how it happened.

Odin wished to acquire the secret of runes, those magical symbols out of which writing grew. But such a secret, which conferred on its owner universal power, could only be won by a terrible sacrifice. He must endure the spiritual and physical torture of hanging by the neck from a bough of the World Ash over the bottomless abyss for nine days and nights. Swung this way and that in the darkness of the inter-galactic winds which drive like rivers of air from the uttermost boundaries of space, Odin, himself a god, the father of the Æsir, was made to howl in terror. At the end of his ordeal the glorious secret of the magic runes was made known to him and ever afterwards he put this wisdom to the service of men and gods.

Odin in all his glory ruled Asgard, the Gods' Enclosure, which he and his sons built above the clouds, supported by Yggdrasill over the centre of Midgard. The palaces of Asgard were buildings of pure delight. First the gods erected Gladsheim or Joyous Home, said to be the finest building ever constructed. Here are to be found their twelve thrones, one higher than the rest for Odin himself. Inside and outside everything was made of burning gold. They built a second mansion as a shrine for the goddesses. It too was very beautiful: men call it Vingolf or Friendly Floor. Their next job was to plan a workshop, for labour with the hands was considered to be an honourable and worthwhile occupation. In the workshop they set a forge and made in addition the first hammer, tongs and anvil, and by means of these all other kinds of tools. They made metal, stone and wood, particularly that metal called gold, enough to have all their utensils and dishes of gold. That's why this time was called the Golden Age.

In the centre of Asgard stretched the smiling plain of Idavale and adorning its hills and valleys their splendid palaces set in smooth green lawns. There was one called Breidablik or Broad Gleaming which had few equals. There was Glitnir the Shining, whose walls and every room and pillar were made of gold, while the thatch was solid silver. Or again, there was a corner called the Hill of Heaven: it stood at the far end of Asgard by the foundation stone of the rainbow bridge – where Bifrost arches out from heaven.

Bifrost, the Tremulous Way, called by more

stolid people the rainbow, was the bridge
built by the gods between Midgard and
Asgard, the road from earth to heaven. It was
and is exceedingly strong in spite of its
frail appearance for it was made with more
artifice and cunning than any other of
the gods' handiwork. All the gods except Thor
ride daily over Bifrost bridge to the well of
Wyrd, where they meet in judgement.
Thor goes there on foot, wading the rivers he
crosses on his way, for the thunder and
lightning that accompany his chariot
on normal journeys would shake the delicate
balance of the bridge. And that will not
happen until the end. Once again High's voice
became full of seriousness as he talked
about the far future.
'Strong as it is,' he said, 'Bifrost will crumble
when the evil fire giants of Muspell cross it,
swimming their stallions through the swollen

rivers; for over Bifrost lies their road
into Asgard. But do not blame the gods for its
weakness: no corner of the universe will
remain unscathed when those terrible times,
the Ragnarok, come upon us.'
 Gylfi shivered and for a long time no-one
said anything else.
 Then 'Is there more to be learned about
Asgard?' he asked at last.
'Much, much more,' growled High, 'but first
you might be interested to hear a little
about Hel. Asgard is a very selective place as
far as mankind is concerned,' he went on
significantly, 'and some information on the
subject of Hel might come in useful to you.'
'I suppose the road leads downwards to Hel,'
remarked King Gylfi.
 Down, always down, plummeting, plunging
down by zig-zag roads clinging to black
vertical cliffs; each further descent enveloped

in gloom, each twist of the track howling with ice-cold winds screaming upwards from Niflheim, the realm of mist and snow. King Gylfi shivered again.

The entrance to Hel, Gnipahellir or Cliff Cave is a grim black hole set among precipitous cliffs and ravines. Snowflakes blow out of it in blizzards. This dark cavern is guarded by a fearsome hound with a bloody chest whose very name is like a growl, Garmr. He is chained to his post, for if he were free he would leap above, ravening wildly around the upper world attacking both men and gods. The blood on the shaggy hair of his chest comes from those who pass him but are so terrified with what they see of Hel that they try to escape back into the world of sunlight.

All roads to the Underworld lead down, whether from Asgard, Midgard or Jotunheim, and not only dead men are to be found there but also the phantoms of gods and giants.

Sinners from Midgard go to Hel, especially oath-breakers, murderers and those who have been disloyal. Those who deserve punishment receive it everlastingly. There is an island in the Underworld called Naastrand, the Corpse Strand, on which stands a great torture chamber, a horrid place of punishment. This hall is always out of reach of sunlight and its doors face the dark north. At first the walls and roof appear to be made of wickerwork, but the plaited bars are not wooden wattles but the entwined bodies of poisonous serpents whose gaping jaws dribble venom from their fangs to burn the sinners crowded underneath. Here are imprisoned the oath-breakers, murderers and adulterers. Some, no doubt, have died a second death on the way to this place, for they have had to wade the terrifying river Slid or Fearful, full not of water but of knives, daggers and sharp swords. They only escape the snake-pit of Naastrand to plunge to Niflhel, nine worlds

down where dead men drop from Hel.

At the wharf by the shore of Naastrand, a dreadful longship is being built. This is Nailfarer Naglfar, the dead men's nail ship, built through all time from the toe and finger nails of those who go to their death without having their nails trimmed. The captain of that vessel (who shall be nameless for the present) will be the greatest sinner of all, unfaithful, disloyal and even indirectly the murderer of a god. He and his grisly crew will fight on the side of the frost giants at the Ragnarok – so all good men who wish to delay that day of doom should see to it that their nails are always neat and short.

The queen of this far flung kingdom is herself called Hel. Her courts are exceedingly vast and are full of the signs of death. Her plate is called Hunger; her knife and fork Famine; Senility is her house-slave and Dotage her bondmaid. At the entrance her doorstep is Pitfall. Her complexion is half livid, half normal; and she is hideous to look at. 'This is a very depressing subject,' said Gylfi. 'Isn't there anybody alive in Hel?'

High told him that *everybody* was alive in Hel. 'If you call zombies or the walking dead alive – but that wouldn't make you any more anxious to meet them alone on a dark night. In addition,' High said, 'some very important personages in Hel are prisoners who have never passed through death but who were banished there by the gods; and that includes the queen herself.

'There are also a handful of people from the upper worlds who have made their way down into Hel and won their way back alive. But all these stories will be related in their proper place.'

'You have told me quite enough about Hel. Now what about Jotunheim?' Gylfi wanted to know.

Jotunheim, the world of the giants, is always a worrying place both for gods and men. When you are surrounded with enemies you cannot help but feel apprehensive, and when those enemies are mountain giants, frost giants and fire giants who are quite likely to gobble up anyone who trespasses in their domains, then apprehension turns to terror. Fortunately, the gods are well prepared both to resist attack by giants on their own stronghold of Asgard and to carry the assault to Jotunheim. It is Thor, of course, who continually keeps them at bay with his famous hammer.

'But', said King Gylfi's informants, 'all these troubles hardly existed in the dawn of time for that, as we have already told you, was called The Golden Age.'

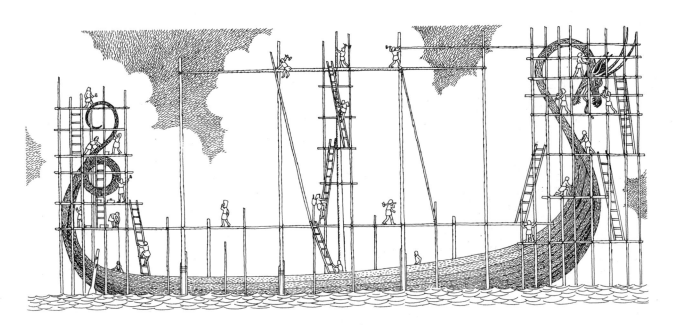

The Golden Age in Asgard

In the morning of time when everything was new and fresh and good, the gods enjoyed their lives in sweet content. Each untroubled day was filled with happiness, the sun rising and setting undisturbed by clouds, with the weather neither too hot nor too cold. At night the sky sparkled with stars until the moon rose and filled the landscape with milky light and soft shadows. In those days the gods and goddesses were able to sleep untroubled with dreams or worries of any kind, past or future, for they were oblivious of Time.

Time was there, but the Æsir were not part of it: Odin was their father and Frigg their mother and the rest of the gods and goddesses made up a happy, young family. When they got up and looked in their golden mirrors they saw the same unchanged likeness as was there the day before, and as would always be in the future. For the gods had access to the secret of eternal youth. This secret reposed in a magic fruit: enchanted apples in the keeping of a flaxen-haired goddess called Idunn. Every day she gave each of the Æsir one of her sharp-sweet apples to eat and as a result they never grew old.

The flowery landscape of Asgard remained at that sweet-scented season when spring is just about to turn into summer. The fields, cropped by woolly sheep and grazed by herds of gentle deep-red cows, resembled smooth green lawns. In between the forest trees the dappled deer flitted like flecks of sunlight. The birds sang from the branches and the wind in the leaves was a passing sigh of contentment. From the mountain tops the cataracts dropped and hung and dropped again like veils of white gossamer; and the blue lakes which reflected their fall were smooth as glass.

The mysterious storytellers told Gylfi that in those far off blissful days just as none of the Æsir recognized Time, they also remained untroubled by that other notion which bothers men today, equality. As a result the younger gods were able to accept a measure of authority and discipline, feeling that such a way of life might indeed be good for the soul.

In his capacity as the father of all, Odin had to watch and

care for his family. To help him with his work he had raised on the topmost peak in Asgard an eagle's eyrie of a palace with a view over all the nine worlds in the Tree.

These nine worlds stretched from Asgard, the world of the Æsir in the topmost branches, to the dead world of Hel far down at the Tree's lowest root. Between were the worlds of the Vanir, the light elves, the dark elves, men, dwarfs, frost and hill giants and the fiery giants of Muspell.

Not all these worlds were as easy to locate as Asgard, Midgard and Hel. The Vanir, a related race of gods about whom there will be more to tell later, lived in their own heaven, called Vanaheim. The light elves lived not far from Asgard, the dark elves on the boundary of the icy region of Niflheim and the dwarfs in holes, caverns and tunnels under the ground.

In the early days of Asgard, Odin used to sit brooding on the throne in his palace eyrie which he called Hlidskialf or High Nest. He was concerned about the affairs of the whole universe and when he sat there he was able to see what everyone was doing and to understand everything he saw. This was not only a tremendous privilege but also a tremendous responsibility and on that account no-one but Odin was allowed to sit on this high seat. Up there the wind whistled as though through resonant organ pipes; when gales blew below on Midgard the people believed that Odin was passing overhead, bringing the wind roaring down from his mountain top.

Odin's constant companions in High Nest were two friendly wolves. Because the father of the gods needed no food himself, he gave the delicacies which stood on the table to the two wolves. It seems that they never refused for their names were Geri Greediguts and Freki Gobble-up. For Odin, wine was both meat and drink.

As he sat brooding over the nine worlds, two ravens named Huginn (Thought) and Muninn (Memory) perched on his shoulders, whispering into his ears every scrap of news which they saw or heard tell of. At crack of dawn every day he pushed them off to flap all round the universe ('I expect you must have seen them,' said High) and they returned in time for breakfast. Much of Odin's information came from them and they are the reason why he is sometimes called the raven god.

Quite often (but this was much later on, when the state of affairs in Asgard had changed radically, some say for the worse) Odin used to go in disguise to visit the other worlds below. On these occasions he appeared as an old, old man apparently blind in one eye, but with his other eye burning so fiercely that it would root an observer to the ground.

Odin was forced to make these journeys because he knew the future: they were his way of preparing for the coming Ragnarok. It was during these journeys of preparation that he adopted so many different names, each of which referred to a twist or turn in the development of his being. 'One-eyed', 'Flame-eyed', 'Masked one', 'Hanged god' were all different ways of describing Odin.

Before Time was forced upon the gods in Asgard they continued to live in happiness, peace and prosperity. Odin's wife, and mother of the Æsir, was Frigg. From High Nest Odin could easily see his wife's palace in the western part of Asgard. It was called Fensalir and was a spacious and airy building full of light. There sat Frigg, surrounded by her handmaidens as she worked with her strong, slim fingers, teasing golden threads between her distaff and her jewelled spinning-wheel to weave later into summer clouds. Her hair hung down in two thick braids as fair and fine as the magic flax she spun. Her face was beautiful but her deep blue eyes were sad: she knew there were sorrows to come. About her there was always the sweet scent of flowers and the luscious ripe odours of the fruits of the earth.

The eldest son of Frigg and Odin was the boisterous god Thor. A red-haired, red-bearded rascal of a god, he always acted first and thought last, a tendency which frequently landed him in trouble.

Thor was the god best loved by the people of Midgard. They enjoyed his rip-roaring passage across their skies in his chariot drawn by two mammoth-sized goats – Toothgnasher and Toothgrinder. At that time the peals of thunder boomed from the wheels of his war-wagon and lightning exploded as he hurled his blazing hammer.

Men loved Thor because he gave them good crops. When his sheet lightning flashed across the fields of heavy-eared corn waiting to turn colour, they said he was ripening the yield; when his fork lightning dazzled the eastern horizon they knew he was hunting trolls and doing battle with the giants. So men called him 'Whip-it-up Thor', and 'Defender of Asgard and Midgard', 'Adversary', 'Slayer of giants and trolls' and especially 'Foe of the Midgard Serpent'.

In addition to his famous hammer, Miolnir the Mullicrusher, Thor also owned a strength-increasing belt. This was perhaps his best treasure, for when he buckled it on, his already enormous strength was doubled. His third precious possession was a pair of iron gauntlets. Without these he could not have grasped his fiery hammer, or caught it when it flew back to him like a boomerang after each throw.

Thor's estate in Asgard was Thruthvangar, the Paddocks of Power, where stood his castle hall Bilskirnir or Lightning. That building had five hundred and forty rooms – the most extensive mansion known to man. Here he lived with his beautiful wife Sif, whose long hair was made of pure gold. She was the goddess of the cornfields and her long, shining hair – which has a story of its own – rippled over her shoulders like the ripening wheat.

Of course it goes without saying that the dining table in Thor's hall Bilskirnir groaned with meat and drink for above all Thor was a startling eater who had been known to finish a whole ox and drink three barrels of mead at one sitting. Even his enemies the giants could not do better than that.

Odin's and Frigg's second son was Balder, a person of very good report indeed.

He stood out even among the Æsir. He was the fairest of the gods, so fair-haired and pale-skinned that a power of light beamed from him. Everyone loved Balder and he himself loved all things, small and large, beautiful and ugly. He lived in Breidablik, the Broad Gleaming Palace with his wife Nanna.

Balder's brother, Hoder, was blind. Later, as we shall see, his blindness was used to bring sadness to all Asgard but for the time being he lived happily enough. Although he could not see the beauty of Asgard, there were plenty of things he could appreciate: the warm rays of the sun, the hundred and one sounds of birds and animals, the speech and music of the other gods. In those days no-one in Asgard was unhappy.

Odin's fourth son was Tyr, a very brave god indeed. There is no doubt that Tyr was the most daring and courageous of all the Æsir and many tales are told about him. Brave warriors on earth carved his rune spell on the handle of their swords and called on his name when they went into battle.

Living in Asgard and counted as one of the Æsir was Heimdall. Men on earth called him the white god and considered him a mighty and holy god but it is not clear where he came from. He was not a son of Odin and it is said that nine women, all sisters, mysteriously gave birth to him. He is sometimes called Gullintanni or Golden Teeth, for his teeth were made of living gold; his horse was called Gold-Topping from its mane of fine gold wires.

Heimdall had his stronghold, a palace that was more of a barbican than a house, at the very edge of Asgard, close to Bifrost bridge. There he stood sentinel, watching out for the giants' assault on the bridge. He could sleep like a bird with one eye open and it is said that his ears could detect the noises made by blades of grass as they grew or the hairs getting longer on a sheep's back.

Slung from a baldrick over his shoulder Heimdall carried at the ready a mighty bugle, Giallarhorn, the alarm horn, whose blasts reached every nook and cranny of all the nine worlds, from highest to lowest.

When the giants cross Bifrost bridge and the Ragnarok begins, Heimdall will blow on Giallarhorn to call the gods and everyone who is on their side to fight against the powers of evil.

Another god, Vidarr, was also preparing for the Ragnarok. Vidarr, a strange, silent god, said to be the next strongest to Thor himself, had charge of a mysterious thing called the Thickmost Shoe. Just as in Hel the nail trimmings of dead men were used to build the dragon longship Naglfar, so in Asgard the ends and snippets of leather thrown away by cobblers on earth were fashioned into a great, thick shoe. When the time for the last battle arrives, Vidarr will pull that magic shoe onto one of his feet to stamp on one of the worst enemies of the gods. If the pieces of leather collected for so long in Midgard prove to have made a shoe big enough and strong enough, all will be well. Otherwise . . . who knows?

In those early days of creation, anyone walking the enchanted lawns of Asgard would have missed certain of the gods and goddesses. Niord, god of the sea, his daughter Freya, goddess of love and his son Frey, god of fertility, had not as yet come to live there. They belonged to the Vanir and were at that time still living in their own world of Vanaheim.

However, wandering about Asgard you would have seen other of the Æsir about whom there are stories to be told. Vali, Odin's son was not born yet but there was Ull, son of Sif and stepson of Thor. He was a famous archer, an expert on skis and a very great warrior. Men called on him for help during duels and in single combat.

The son of Balder and his wife Nanna was called Forseti. He lived in Glitnir, the Shining Palace and was held to be the best judge who ever lived either in a quarrel or when a problem was apparently insoluble. Anyone who applied to him for help left with peace of mind.

There was Bragi, too, a god celebrated for his eloquence and skill with words, a great poet. In fact poetry was often called 'Bragi's breath' after him. His wife was the goddess Idunn, keeper of the ashwood casket containing the magic apples which enabled the gods to retain their eternal youth.

Odin's brothers Hoenir and Lothur also still lived in Asgard as did the mysterious god Mimir whose severed head was later the source of all the knowledge of all time, past, present and future. In the early days, however, he lived as the other gods, in peace and prosperity.

Some of the old books describe the World Ash Tree as Mimir's Tree or Mimir's Wood, showing how important and powerful a god Mimir must once have been. He is also sometimes called Treasure-Mimir a name which recalls the days when he was not only wise but a famous smith who created treasures for the gods.

During this Golden Age, the Æsir enjoyed happy married lives. Frigg, Sif, Idunn and Nanna have already been mentioned. Later, other goddesses came to live with their husbands in Asgard. Gerda and Skadi were two giant maidens, who were taken in to the world of the gods. It is said that when Gerda, a woman of surpassing beauty, lifted the door latch of her home, a light was reflected over all the northern sky. As for Skadi, she was forever out on snowshoes or skis, hunting animals with her bow and arrows. She is often referred to as the snowshoe goddess, or the goddess on skis.

Before she married into Asgard, her home was in the icy mountains and frozen fiords where the cracking, creaking glaciers calve exploding icebergs, a northern region which is well named Thrumheim, the Home of Clamour.

'Isn't there somebody you've forgotten?' King Gylfi asked after the three had been silent for a while.

Their eyes blazed and Gylfi suddenly felt frightened. The personage who said his name was High said, 'No paradise is without its serpent. There is also counted among the heavenly powers one whom some call the Mischief Maker of the gods, the first father of lies. He is a living shame to everyone whether mortal or divine. His true name is Loki – some call him Loptr – son of the giant Farbauti.

'Loki is handsome but inside he is the soul of spite and fickleness. He is eternally getting the gods into trouble and quite often he pulls them out again with his crafty advice. But no more of him for the present. We have said nothing about the world of men for too long. Now let us see what happened to the descendants of Ash and Elm.'

Heimdall in Midgard

In the early days of creation, when all was pleasant and peaceful in Asgard and nobody really believed that hill or frost giants would ever attack their citadel, Heimdall, the watchman of the gods, sometimes felt very bored. He was therefore delighted when Odin gave him permission to stand down from his post by the Bifrost bridge. It was a chance Heimdall had long been waiting for because he was eager to visit Midgard and play some part in people's lives there. So he put his bugle Giallarhorn and his sword safely away in his castle, left his horse in the care of his grooms, dressed in suitable clothes to hide the fact that he was a god, and set out on foot down the bridge.

In this disguise he trudged across Midgard until he reached a deserted shore. A little way above the high-tide mark, in a cave in the cliff wall, lived a hoary old couple of human beings called Ai (or Greatgrandad) and Edda (or Greatgrandma). Their living conditions were miserable with no furniture but flat rocks to sit on and dried bladderwrack on the cave floor for a bed. Their clothes were the skins of wild animals and they did not know the use of fire.

In spite of their poverty, Ai and Edda welcomed the stranger and offered him food (limpets from the rocks and snails from under the bushes); and to drink, fresh cold water from a nearby spring. Heimdall was touched by their innocent kindliness and asked if they would shelter him for three days. Ai at once said 'Yes'. But Edda had misgivings because there was only one bed of seaweed. Nevertheless it was agreed that the stranger should sleep in the middle, which Edda said was the softest place.

After staying for three nights, Heimdall called Ai and Edda into the cave from their morning task of gathering food. He had a flat piece of driftwood in front of him on the cave floor and between his palms a wooden rod, pointed at the bottom end. He directed the point of the rod into a cup-shaped hollow in the wood, round which he had heaped dry tinder. Then he briskly rubbed his palms backwards and forwards making the rod turn so that the friction at its point quickly produced smoke and soon afterwards the magic flower which men now call fire.

Ai and Edda jumped back in amazement, but they soon learned what benefits Heimdall had bestowed on them with this gift of fire. Nine months later (when they had almost forgotten the stranger's visit) Edda gained a second gift from Heimdall, for she gave birth to a son.

Edda's son had black hair and they named him Thrall. He grew into a big hulk of a fellow, with wrinkled rough skin, knotted knuckles, a twisted back and an ugly face. When he was old enough Thrall married a young woman similar in appearance to himself. Her name was Serf; she was bow-legged with calloused feet, sunburned arms and a flat nose. Before long they had a very large family. All the children worked every day about the house or outside herding geese, pigs and goats, muck-spreading, digging turf, hedging and ditching according to the ways of serving folk. They were the ancestors of the thralls.

After Heimdall had left the miserable hovel of Ai and Edda he came to a respectable house where lived Afi (Grandad) and Amma (Granny). As Heimdall came up to the door, Afi was using an adze to pare wooden beams, the shavings flying about like large snowflakes. Heimdall offered his help and between them they constructed a loom.

Afi was neat and tidy with a trim beard and hair curling tightly over his forehead. His clothes were clean and fitted well. His wife Amma sat contentedly by the open fireplace with a spinning wheel and distaff.

At supper time Afi and Amma offered Heimdall a meal of stewed calves' flesh and a dish of skyr, a sort of curds without the whey. When bedtime came there arose the same problem as with Ai and Edda: there was only one bed. Once again Heimdall had to make do with a naked bedmate on either side of him.

Nine months after the god had passed by, Amma bore a son whom the surprised father and happy mother called Karl the Yeoman.

Karl had a rosy face and sparkling eyes. He grew up to own oxen and ploughs, to make carts and build houses and barns. Karl's bride was a competent housewife, with the keys to every cupboard jingling from a girdle at her waist. The running of the household was a well-ordered business of which she took full charge. Her name was Daughter-in-Law. Karl and Daughter-in-Law also had many children: from these are descended the race of yeoman farmers.

A third time as he passed through Midgard, Heimdall paid an unexpected visit, this time to a couple simply called Father and Mother, who lived in a castle. When Heimdall arrived Father was twisting strings for his hunting bow and shaving rods for spears. Mother had little to do except look beautiful. She was wearing a blue silk gown with a broad train, jewelled brooches on her breast and an embroidered cap. They welcomed Heimdall graciously and invited him to feast with them at a table covered with a brightly patterned cloth. There were thin loaves of bread, well-cooked meat and game in silver dishes, and horns of wine.

When night came Heimdall slept between Father and Mother in a fine, large bed with cool white linen sheets. After the third night he thanked them both profusely and returned to Asgard and his sentry post at the end of Bifrost bridge.

Nine months after Heimdall's visit Mother gave birth to a blond haired, bright cheeked baby with fierce, proud eyes. They called him Jarl the Earl and as he grew he spent his time with lances and shields, bows and arrows; he learned to handle a sword, to hunt with hawk and hounds and to swim. When Jarl was a young man, Heimdall came again to Midgard, to visit this earthly son. The god told him of his high lineage, gave him one of his own nicknames, Regal, and claimed him for his son.

Regal grew up to be a ruler of men. His wife, Erna the Proud, bore him many sons and one, named King the Young, was the first of a line of kings destined to rule forever – or at least until the Ragnarok.

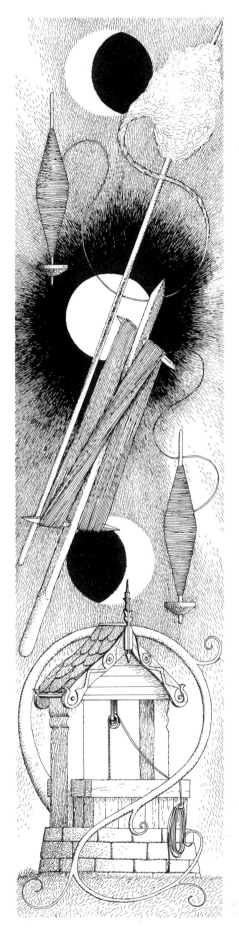

The Norns

For some reason, King Gylfi's informants did not seem to want to tell him very much about the Norns, the three strange sisters who sat by the Asgard root, tending the well of Wyrd. Gylfi could not understand it. Several times he had started to ask about them but as soon as he opened his mouth the three looked distinctly apprehensive and changed the subject abruptly.
The sisters seemed to have some sort of hold over even the gods. Perhaps witchcraft was at the bottom of it. They were apparently so all-powerful that it was better to talk about them in whispers and even then to cast an occasional glance over your shoulder: as if Destiny might be creeping up behind you.

The truth is that the arrival of the three women in Asgard had radically altered the Æsirs' way of life. The Norns had staked a claim to a far-off, secluded region of Asgard, down under the first root of the World Ash Yggdrasill. Their dwelling was a dark cave in front of which bubbled a round, white well, almost like a full moon on the ground. About it, in a patterned maze, twisted the firm root of the tree. Every day the three sisters came from their cave and sat by the well and the root. No-one ever described their faces, for they were hidden in the shadows of their cloudy shawls. Were they young and beautiful or old and withered? Nobody knew. Every morning the three sisters scooped water from their spring to mix with the magic clay and gravel around its banks: this made the powerful, holy paste which they spread over the root to stop any rotting and so preserve the life of the whole tree.

The sisters came originally from Jotunheim, the land of the giants. They were sisters (so it seemed) to Narfi, one of the first giants to live there. Narfi, you will remember, was the father of Night and the three sisters were also connected with darkness and the moon in its three phases of waxing, full and waning.

Every morning, after they had tended the Tree's root, the sisters began to spin. But the thread they spun was no ordinary thread: on it hung the lives not only of every person and every god who was ever born, but also the destiny of the universe itself. For they were the people who measured Time, controlling past, present and future as they spun.

It was from this work that they took their names: Wyrd, the oldest sister, means Becoming, Verdandi, the middle one, means Being and Skuld, the youngest, means That-which-is-to-be. Their collective name, the Norns, means the Fates.

King Gylfi pictured them crouched above their whirring spinning wheel, hunched over the lengthening thread, measuring it out and – snip-snap! – cutting it. He shuddered as he realized that their spinning was a job which, once begun, nobody could stop. They had introduced Time into the scheme of things and once started, Time can never be stopped, never be turned back. This, of course, was why the Æsir were so apprehensive of the work the Norns did. As soon as they arrived in Asgard, the timeless existence of the youthful gods in the Golden Age stopped. From that moment, their growing old could only be delayed. Idunn's apples would keep them artificially young for a time but if ever these apples were stolen away, the Æsir, the gods themselves, would age and fail. Now that Time and Fate had come to Asgard, a sequence of events must take place one after the other until the crack of doom. Nothing could prevent the inevitable end.

The Norns' home by the well, in the shadow of the Tree root, became a holy place. It was holy for three reasons: it was there that the root was tended and preserved so that no rot could spread through the universe; it was there that Wyrd, Verdandi and Skuld spun the thread of life and death; and it was there that the Æsir went every day to deliberate in sacred council, to make plans to delay for as long as possible their own doom and the destruction of their world.

No-one except the gods could reach that far corner of Asgard. Part of their way lay over the rainbow bridge. The journey was long and difficult, especially for Thor, who could not ride his chariot across the bridge but was forced to wade through four turbulent rivers before he reached the well of Wyrd.

But Thor was used to struggle. From the time the Norns arrived the struggle between the powers of good and evil would never cease until the Ragnarok and Thor the Thunderer was from the start one of the most enthusiastic fighters.

'The task of the gods is not an easy one,' said one of the three, raising his voice above a whisper for the first time in a long while. 'And it was made all the more difficult because the one who is the very essence of evil succeeded in worming his way into the home of the gods. His name is Loki.'

Loki and his evil children

There lived among the Æsir a mischief maker called Loki. In face and form he was bewitchingly handsome, except for his shifty eyes – they gave him away. His soul looked out from his eyes and that was black, fickle and full of spite with a talent for slyness and for knowing a cunning trick for all occasions.

You might wonder how he came to be in Asgard at all, and it has to be admitted that Odin found it attractive, exciting to play with evil just as some children find excitement in playing with fire. Loki was like fire in many ways – beautiful to look at but if you put your finger to it, it burns you. In the early days of Asgard, Loki was the gods' fire: they played with him for a long time but in the end they got burned.

Loki was another one of those from giant stock. His father was a giant called Farbauti who controlled dangerous lightning, the blazing ball-lightning. He fathered other fearful sons including Whirlwind and Waterspout. They say Loki's mother was Laufey which means Tree Island or Bushy Tree Top and they think that she gave birth to Loki when Farbauti's ball-lightning struck her. The fireball probably burned her to a charred and smoking ember; at least nothing is heard of her again. This must have taken place in one of the forests in a remote part of Asgard, for when Loki arrived at Odin's hall, the father of the Æsir welcomed him as he would any long distance traveller. Loki was so handsome and his ways so winning that Odin in time actually became his blood-brother. It was believed that when blood was mixed from wrist to wrist the tie was stronger than that of brotherhood by birth.

The exploits of Loki in Asgard and Jotunheim gained him many nicknames by which he is always remembered with disgust. They include Evil Boon Companion of the Æsir, the Sly God, Thief of Sif's Hair, Thief of Idunn's Apples, and many more. All these names came from one or other of his exploits, and all of them were disgraceful. But occasionally he got into a situation which could only make people laugh.

Loki's children were even more terrible than he was himself. His wife in Asgard was Sigyn, but he had three children by an ogress from Jotunheim called Angrbode. Like Loki it seemed that Angrbode was a mixture of beauty and sin, for two of her other names are Gold Might and Shining. While she was at home in Jotunheim Angrbode had had a daughter who was surpassingly beautiful. Her name was Gerda and as we shall see, the god Frey was to fall in love with her.

King Gylfi said, 'The family relationships of the Æsir, Loki and the giants seem rather surprising and complicated.'
'Family relationships are always surprising,' replied his informants. 'People like to show a respectable face to the world, but most families have a skeleton hidden away in the cupboard.'
'I hardly expected that the Æsir would have anything to hide,' observed Gylfi. His informants quickly showed him how wrong he was.

The gods eventually banished Angrbode to the Ironwood, that dark and dismal forest far to the east of Midgard where few would know of her existence. There Angrbode gave birth to Loki's first monstrous son, the wolf Fenrir. In the beginning, because Loki was his father, the Æsir allowed the wolf cub to be brought up in Asgard. Later on they discovered their mistake.

Soon the surprising news reached Asgard from Ironwood that Angrbode had littered a second monstrous son, this time a mighty serpent, a dragon so colossal that his coils split the trees apart and before long he had encircled the whole of Midgard. Odin quickly called up all his reserves of divine power and cast the serpent into the sea, condemning him to wallow forever with his tail gripped between his jaws. That stopped him from growing. They do say that sailors blown far out of sight of land by contrary winds have sometimes clapped eyes on the World Serpent or Jormungander (as he came to be called); and some, thinking one of his huge coils was an uncharted island, have cast anchor into his hide, scrambled 'ashore' and even lit a fire on the monster's back. It was only when the island suddenly disappeared from under their feet, leaving them astonished and struggling in the waves that the sailors understood that they had run into the World Serpent and been lucky enough to live to tell the tale.

Yet a third time Angrbode gave birth, on this occasion to a female child whom Odin cast down into the Underworld to become queen of Hel. She was given the name of Hel and made absolute ruler over any people of the nine worlds who came into her power.

Angrbode's daughter, the lovely maiden Gerda, continued for the time being to live in Jotunheim with her father Gymir. She was as good as she was beautiful but even she could not avoid the taint of evil passed on by her mother. Through no fault of her own she was to bring misfortune to all the Æsir.

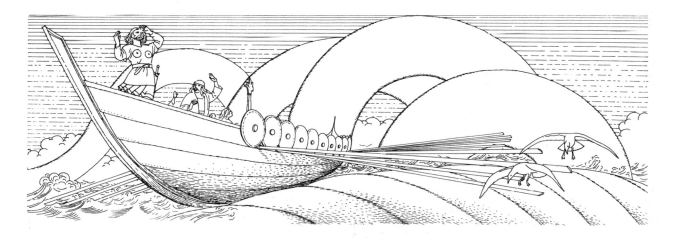

War in heaven

The Vanir were a very important race of gods.
'Yes, who were they?' asked Gylfi, 'Their origins seem to be a bit mysterious and how exactly do they fit in with the Æsir?'

High said, 'There's nothing odd about their origins; they lived in Vanaheim to the east of Asgard and they came to be closely related to the Æsir by marriage and adoption. The world of Vanaheim is high in the branches of Yggdrasill and its borders run up to Asgard.'

The most important of the Vanir was Niord, a seafaring god, always jolly when he was among boats and busy harbours, a deity with a definite liking for the salt smell of the ocean and the pungent odour of pitch. His home in heaven was right on the coast at Noatun, near the shipyards where he could hear not only the gulls but the merry noise of busy adzes, saws and awls in the hands of shipwrights working on oak planking. He loved to watch the cat's cradle the skilled rope-walkers created as they twisted rigging for the merchant vessels and longships. He was the favourite of mariners and deepsea fishermen who called on him when they needed help since he had power over wind and waves and could dowse fire – always a hazard at sea.

Niord's second wife was Skadi, daughter of the giant Thiazzi. Skadi did not like the sea. She was determined to set up house in the mountains among her noisy kinfolk at Thrumheim. The happy pair had to come to terms, agreeing to spend one week by the sea and the next in the mountains, turn and turn about. When Niord came back from his first week on the fells he cried: 'How I hated those noisy mountains. I was only there a week and the howling wolves nearly drove me out of my mind. What I wouldn't have given just to hear the music of the gannet!'

And Skadi retorted: 'Music! Personally, I couldn't sleep a wink on the bed of the sea! The kittiwakes saw to that – they were worse than serenading cats. No sooner did I close my eyes than they were opened again by the bawling herring-gulls' squawking!'

Niord by his first marriage had twins, the god Frey and the goddess Freya. The brother and sister were both very beautiful and exceedingly powerful when they grew up, exercising sway over all that grows.

Wherever they went, plants, flowers and trees lifted up their heads and flourished, crops ripened, farm animals thrived and were fertile, and young men and women turned their thoughts to love.

The trouble all began with a prank when some of the Vanir were visiting Asgard and Frey got into mischief. While the parents were talking about this and that (a subject quite boring to Frey) the young fellow sneaked up to Odin's forbidden High Nest, sat down on the throne and was able to see over the whole universe.

It was an exciting moment until, glancing across the vistas to the north, his eyes caught sight of a town where a magnificent dwelling stood. A maiden was walking towards it. As she raised her hands to unlatch the door in front of her, a beautiful light shone from them so that earth and sea and sky were brighter for it. Frey paid dearly for his pride in wanting to sit in the High Seat, reserved only for the father of the gods: he now staggered away love-sick at heart. On arriving back home in Vanaheim he locked himself in his palace and would speak to no-one. He would not eat nor drink and nobody knew what to do about it.

The situation rapidly became serious because all Nature began to fail in sympathy with the ailing god.

At last, his father had Frey's boyhood friend and servant Skirnir called to him and ordered him to go to Frey and ask what was the matter with him.

Skirnir said he would go if he must, but he was not eager; he didn't believe it would do any good. He found Frey lying on his ornate bed carved with twisted vine tendrils and bunches of grapes. He was looking vacantly up at the rafters. Outside the window the dead leaves drifted down from the trees and the flowers in the garden had withered. Skirnir said, 'They want me to ask you why you are so glum?'

Frey was slow to answer. 'I can't tell anyone why I'm languishing, my heart is so

heavy and the subject too painful to discuss.'

Skirnir reminded Frey how as lads they had always shared each other's secrets. 'Nobody can help you if you don't say what is wrong,' he said.

'No-one can help me if I do tell,' said Frey, 'because not only Odin and my father will be against what I want, but the elves will be against it too.'

'Whatever can it be that so many powerful people will oppose?' asked Skirnir.

At last Frey said, 'Because of our friendship I'll tell you. I want Gerda the daughter of the ogress Angrbode and the giant Gymir to be my wife. Since I saw her from Odin's High Seat I cannot live without her. And now you are here I want you to ride to Jotunheim and demand her hand in marriage for me.'

Skirnir was shocked. 'I hear she is surpassingly beautiful,' he said, 'but her father is a frightful ogre and her mother is worse. You know they would never consent to let her leave Jotunheim.'

'Under certain conditions they will,' said Frey, 'but impossible conditions, and that is why it's hopeless and why I'm languishing and shall do so until I die – which won't be long now.'

The thought of Frey's death only made matters worse, for if the god of fertility and love died, all Nature would die too.

Skirnir asked, 'What are the conditions?'

Frey said, 'The giants want my sword as a bride-price.'

It was one shock after another. Frey's magic sword had the property of being able to fight of its own accord. It must do battle for the gods if they were to have any success when the evil fire giants galloped against them at the Ragnarok. That was the express purpose for which the sword had been forged with such powerful spells by the light elves.

Skirnir gulped. 'But even if I took your sword,' he said, 'there's no guarantee that I should survive the dangerous journey or succeed in entering Gymir's stronghold which you know is fenced about by magic flickering flames – an impassable barrier.'

'Impassable to every steed but one,' said Frey,

'Odin's stallion can do it. You must borrow him.'

Skirnir nearly fainted. The enormity of what Frey was asking him to do literally took his breath away, winding him like a blow. He looked out of the window as if for help but all he saw was that Nature was dying. Skirnir was a brave lad.

'I can see there isn't any choice,' he said. 'I'll do it. I shall have to steal the horse secretly for a time and hope I'm not found out. I will take your magic sword with me but I'll try to win Gerda without having to give it up. There's no choice,' he repeated to himself. More leaves fluttered down from the trees outside. 'Even now I may be too late.'

That night when the Æsir were sleeping, Skirnir put muffles on Odin's horse's hooves and led him from his stable. He leaped onto the stallion's back and galloped through the air to Jotunheim. From far away the flames surrounding Gymir's mountain stronghold guided him as the North Star does the sailor. When he drew near he saw the fires were like a blazing stockade. The horse did not falter; he collected himself before the daunting obstacle, gave a mighty leap upwards and flew through the air. Skirnir smelled the singeing of horsehair as the flames swirled towards the horse's flying tail. Then they landed safely in the giant's courtyard.

'Who's this who comes walloping through the upper air?' growled a voice. It was the giant Gymir. 'Are you one of the Æsir, the Vanir or the elves?'

'My name is Skirnir. I am not of the Æsir, the Vanir or the elves. I come from Frey. The young god asks for the hand of your daughter Gerda in marriage.'

Gerda was at her chamber window, which was all lit up from within. She heard what was going on and asked, 'What does Frey offer as a dowry?'

Skirnir said he could get eleven golden apples. Gerda said she did not want them.

He said he might be able to procure a magic ring from which eight others dropped every ninth night. Gerda answered that she had enough treasure in gold of her own.

Skirnir tried threats. He drew Frey's sword and shouted up to the window that if she did not agree he would cut off her head. Gerda answered that her father would prevent it. Skirnir said that Gymir would be doomed to die before the blade which, once given the order, fought of its own accord. She remained unmoved. Skirnir told the brave maiden that he owned a magic wand which would cast a spell over her, constraining her to do his will. He threatened her with dire consequences. He would force her to go to the Eagle's Hill overlooking Hel, where all her food would become loathsome and disgusting to her as she lay in the power of the frost giant Rimer. She would have to endure madness, longing, fetters, wrath, tears and torment.

'You mean I shall fall in love?' she taunted him.

'I will put you in the power of the three-headed frost giant Rime-Mask in the depths by the Corpse Gate,' he cried. 'Every day you will be compelled to crawl to the frost giant's hall and beg for mercy in vain and without any hope. Under the root of Yggdrasill which stretches towards the frost giants, evil thralls will force you to drink the water of goats.'

Skirnir's voice rose to a scream as he cried that he would put a curse on Gerda by cutting four terrible runes as a spell to bring upon her longing, madness and lust.

'The bride price is still Frey's sword,' said Gerda.

Gymir said, 'My daughter is too steadfast, too brave to be moved by your threats. If she wasn't, she would hardly be a suitable wife for Frey. As she says, there is only one bride-price, the same as it always was – the magic sword of Frey.'

Skirnir realized that he had lost the struggle and handed over the sword. He made arrangements for the marriage. Then he rode back to Asgard and slipped Odin's horse into his stable as dawn was breaking. He returned to Vanaheim and to Frey.

'Gerda has agreed to marry you,' he said dejectedly, 'but I had to hand over your sword.

The Æsir will be wrathful and the
elves too, for they forged it for you alone.'
'Where and when is this wedding to be?'
gasped Frey.
'At the island of Barleycorn; she said you
both knew where it was. She will meet you
there in three days.'
Then Frey sang a song. It was rather a sad
song but it showed that he was beginning to
recover and with his recovery all Nature
would be saved:

'One night is long.
Another is worse!
How shall I thole for three?
Often a month seemed
shorter to me
than half this night to my wedding.'

So Frey and Gerda were married and began
to live very happily together.

While Frey was particularly concerned
with Nature, having power over the rain and
sunshine, together with the natural increase
of the earth, Freya, his twin sister, was
the goddess of love. Her palace, which was
spacious and airy, was called the Rich-in-
Seats. Everybody was welcome there. She
herself journeyed about quite a lot, sitting in
a trap drawn by a pair of cats as large as
lions. Her husband was sometimes called Ottar.

He frequently went away on long
journeys and when Freya used to weep for him
her tears were all red gold. She was very fond
of precious gems and especially of her famous
necklace, called Brisingamen after the dwarf
tribe, the Brisings, who made it. Freya
even named her daughter Hnoss which means
Jewel.

This little family of Niord, Frey, Gerda and
Freya lived amicably in Vanaheim, occasionally
visiting the Æsir in Asgard until one day a
dreadful quarrel broke out. It was so rancorous
that it resulted in a war between the Æsir
and Vanir – the worst kind of war, civil war,
where relations are set against each other.
Like most wars its causes were obscure and
difficult to disentangle but seemed to lie
in the events just mentioned, namely the affair
of Frey's sitting in Odin's High Seat, his
marriage to Gerda and the loss of his sword.

Odin was furious when he learned how his
horse had been appropriated. He was even
more enraged when he knew that the giants
now possessed Frey's sword, for he could
see into the future and understood what the
consequences would be. The Æsir believed
that the whole train of events had been set in
motion by Gerda's mother Angrbode.

As we have seen, Angrbode had many

names, not all of them with unpleasant meanings. To possess so many different names indicated that she was a shape-changer, and therefore a witch. Witches were, like werwolves and vampires, totally evil and almost impossible to destroy. There was only one way to be rid of a witch – to burn her alive.

'Time in Asgard is sometimes confusing,' said Gylfi. 'I thought this witch-giant had been banished long since to Ironwood.'

'And with a little patience you will find out how she got there,' replied High sharply.

The Æsir invited the witch Angrbode to feast in Asgard. She came in her most beautiful shape, the one in which she was named 'Gold Might'. The gods remarked to each other on her terrible beauty, like nothing they had seen before except in one person, Loki. Her funeral feast (for that is what the gods intended it to be) was held in Valhalla. The loaded tables ran the length of the hall on the raised platform either side of the longfire. When the last course had been eaten and the last drink drunk, the Æsir took the witch and meted out to her the only final punishment for sorcery. They burned her alive, ceremonially, spitting her at the apex of an arch of spears which they held over the longfire.

Witches, however, are not so easily disposed of. Though carbonized, Angrbode was not destroyed but came alive again at once, hissing and spitting with rage.

Twice they burned her and twice she lived. At the third attempt, Loki found her still living heart among the ashes of her body and swallowed it. Then, feeling the enormity of its evil working within him, Loki rushed out of Valhalla, out of Asgard and hid himself in the dark, desolate Ironwood. There, the evil heart, working inside the evil Loki, fertilized him and he and she gave birth to the wolf Fenrir. From Fenrir sprang all the race of wolves, including those who were to chase the sun and the moon across the sky. 'Later, as we told you,' said one of the three, 'the World Serpent and Hel were also born to the witch.'

When the Vanir heard how the Æsir had murdered Angrbode they met in solemn conclave with the gods of Asgard and demanded restitution. It did not matter that Angrbode was a witch whom everybody, including the Vanir, had regarded as evil; in another shape she was also Gerda's mother. Now, with the wedding of Frey and Gerda she had become a relative by marriage to the Vanir and according to the ancient code they were bound to avenge her death. It was the old code of an eye for an eye, a tooth for a tooth. The least the Vanir could do was to demand a body ransom for the witch's death. This the Æsir refused to pay. The argument became hot and angry on both sides until at last Odin put a stop to it by flinging his spear over the heads of the assembled company. It was a declaration of war.

So followed the first of all wars and sadly enough, in heaven. Both sides were equally matched and sometimes the Æsir appeared to be winning, sometimes the Vanir. Asgard walls were breached and extensively broken but the Vanir were driven out. At last when both parties were thoroughly weakened, it occurred to the wiser among them that the frost and fire giants could at any moment walk into both Asgard and Vanaheim and meet with little opposition. So they came to their senses and declared an armistice.

The Æsir held a second solemn conclave, this time to patch up a peace. The gods talked, listened and talked again.

At the end of their deliberations it was agreed that the two sides should exchange hostages as a pledge of good behaviour. As a result, two of the Æsir, the gods Mimir and Hoenir went to live in Vanaheim and Niord, his two children Frey and Freya and Gerda made their home in Asgard.

There's a curious story told about the peace conference. To seal the truce the Æsir and Vanir spat into a jar. When they were leaving, the gods would not allow the peace token to be lost but made a man out of their combined spittle. He was called Kvasir, and was the wisest man who ever lived. He was so wise, in fact, that nobody could ask a question which he was not able to answer. Kvasir went to live in Asgard.

Mimir, one of the two Æsir who went to Vanaheim, was a god of great wisdom.

However, the Vanir soon suspected that Hoenir was less gifted. At their conferences when any difficult subject was debated and Mimir was not at his side, Hoenir always answered in the same way: 'Let somebody else advise on this matter.'

The Vanir felt that the Æsir had deceived them in the exchange of hostages. Angrily they took Mimir, cut off his head and sent it to the Æsir.

As soon as Odin received the head he smeared it with magic herbs to keep it alive and sang powerful spells over it. In this way he made it possible for Mimir's wisdom to continue to be available when the gods were in trouble and needed advice. At those perilous times Odin would consult Mimir's head and the head would open its lips and speak to him.

Wisdom is not easily bought: on the contrary it is only won through sacrifice. Mimir's head was stationed down under the root of Yggdrasill which twists towards the frost giants. They say that the water of the well there confers wisdom and that every morning the head used to drink from it. When Odin first journeyed to the root and asked to share Mimir's wisdom he was told he could only do this if he gave up one of his eyes.

To Odin this exchange was a just one and that is why, when he travels about the world of men in disguise, he passes himself off as an old bearded tramp with only one eye.

The walls of Asgard

Shortly after the war in heaven the Æsir were sadly inspecting the ruined walls of Asgard when a sturdy looking fellow came up leading a magnificent stallion. Nobody had set eyes on him before or knew who he was.

'I see you've got a bit of trouble here,' he said, 'you need a builder.'

This remark did not much please the gods who looked at the stranger down their noses in silence.

'I'll tell you what,' he went on, 'I'm a master mason. I myself will build you your walls in a jiffy – in three seasons in fact, and that's a promise.'

The Æsir still were not impressed. Tyr said, 'The walls we want have to be a rampart completely encircling Asgard and they must be proof against both hill trolls and giants.'

'Then I'm your man,' said the mason, 'and the price isn't dear.'

'How much?' asked Odin.

'The hand of the goddess Freya in marriage – oh, and you can throw in the sun and moon.'

The gods shouted with rage and all began arguing at once, but Odin called them to one side and said they ought to discuss the proposition calmly. Everyone agreed that the price demanded was out of the question. Loki the Mischief Maker said, 'No, wait. Let's tell him we agree to the price . . .'

The Æsir shouted him down till Odin ordered, 'Let him have his say.'

'My suggestion is,' said Loki, 'that we agree to the price but set such hard conditions that he won't be able to fulfil them; and then we can slide out of our side of the bargain.'

'Well, that's only business,' said some of the gods, and so they agreed to try it.

They turned back to the mason and Odin told him that he could build the walls and he should get the price he asked for provided he could finish the work in only one season instead of three. If, by the first day of summer, the last of the stones was unfaced even, then the payment as agreed would be off.

The mason scratched his nose and glanced thoughtfully at his horse who was cropping the greensward with a pleasant munching sound.

'One season eh?' said the Mason. 'Instead of three. You drive a hard bargain. Tell you what: I'll do it provided you allow me to get a little assistance from my nag here.'

Once again the gods fell to arguing and once again Loki's advice weighted the beam and the Æsir agreed that the mason must do all the work himself with no help from anybody except his horse.

The mason worked out the foundations of the walls on the first day of winter, and that same night put his horse in traces, drove him down to the quarries and began hauling up massive boulders. The gods were quite put out next morning to see what mountainous rocks that animal could drag, for it seemed the horse was doing twice as much again of the superhuman task as the mason was. Moreover, while the mason had appeared to be casual when he first named his price, when it came to striking the bargain he had insisted on binding oaths and reputable witnesses. From his point of view this was essential. He was a shape-changer and indeed a giant in disguise so it was more than his life was worth for him to be among the Æsir without a safe-conduct. Before he turned up in Asgard the giant had in addition made quite sure that Thor was not at home. In fact the red-bearded god was travelling about the east hunting trolls.

As winter melted away, the stronghold was nearly done and was now so lofty and stout as to be impregnable: it could not possibly have been taken by storm. The hill giants and frost giants would surely never be able to get into Asgard even if they managed to cross the ocean and infiltrate Midgard.

So the gods were in two frames of mind at once: they were pleased beyond all measure at the success of the construction but worried out of their wits at the thought of the price they would have to pay. They hurriedly called an extraordinary meeting.

As they sat in their judgement seats scratching their heads to know what to do next, somebody asked how they had managed to get themselves into such a pickle.

'I was all in favour of having the rampart built,' said Tyr, 'but I don't remember that I was in favour of the price.'

'Nor I, nor I,' said several of the other gods. Loki looked into a corner.

'Who was it then?' asked Odin, 'who persuaded us against our better judgement to deliver up Freya, loveliest of our young goddesses, and utterly to destroy the sky and heavens by allowing the sun and moon to be snatched away?'

All heads were turned towards Loki, the one who was notorious for giving evil advice, and everybody started shouting at once, reminding each other that Loki had also persuaded them to accept the condition giving the mason the use of his horse.

'Now then,' said Heimdall (always ready to stand out against Loki) 'let him think up another trick to get us out of our dilemma. If he can't, then we should kill him.' Some of the Æsir nearest to Loki had already begun to lay rough hands on him and for once he became very frightened.

'Leave it to me,' he cried, 'leave it to me! I'll see to it the fellow fails.'

'You'd better,' said Heimdall 'or you'll finish up in chains down under the Corpse Gate.'

Loki was very much afraid and he swore mighty oaths that, whatever the cost to

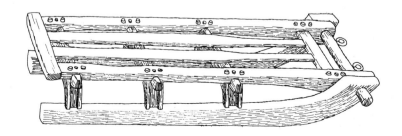

himself, he would arrange things so that the mason should forfeit his fee.

That same evening when the mason drove off for stones with his stallion, who, by the way was called Svadilfari, there trotted out of the forest a dainty looking mare who whinnied at the work horse.

Svadilfari stopped in his tracks. His ears pricked up, his eyes bulged till the whites showed and his haunches trembled.

The mason was no fool but he was just not quick enough. Svadilfari had recognized the horse for a mare and in a flash he had snapped his traces, leaving the giant looking down at the broken reins in his hands. In the shadow of the wood the mare tossed her head and skittered away under the trees with the stallion galloping after her as fast as he could go. You can well imagine that the mason was not far behind either. But no matter how swiftly that giant ran he was never able to catch up with the horse.

All that night the two horses stayed away and the building had to stop for the time being. There were now only three days left to summer and the job was done apart from finishing touches to the fortress gate.

Dawn came but without the horse no work could go on. All that day the mason scoured the wood searching in vain for sight or sound of Svadilfari.

At the end of the second day the Æsir looked down from their new walls and began to feel a little less uneasy. They watched the full moon rise and believed they could once more enjoy, without anxiety, the beauty of the night sky. Soon there was only a day to go before the mason's time limit was up and although the unfinished touches to the already massive construction were almost unnoticeable from the point of view of defence they were quite enough to make him break his side of the bargain.

Judge then, the gods' dismay when on the morning of the last day they saw the triumphant mason leading his stallion back to work in the quarries. His chase had ended.

The Æsir glanced anxiously up at the golden sun and even more anxiously over their shoulders towards Freya's palace, the Rich-in-Seats.

Tomorrow there would be no sun or moon in the sky and no Freya in Asgard. They looked over the walls in the direction of the quarries. The mason had harnessed his stallion to the last huge boulder and was whipping the poor beast for all he was worth. Svadilfari was a sorry sight. His head hung low and his legs were no stronger than jelly. The mason could have flogged him all day without getting him to move. Whatever had happened to him during his truancy he was now as weak as water. He flopped to the ground on his belly.

When the mason realized that he would not finish his task in the agreed time he dropped all pretence, changed back to his true shape and flung into a giant's rage. When the Æsir saw that they had been deceived all along, they paid little respect to their solemn oaths. They shouted loudly for Thor who came back from the east in a flash of lightning and a rumble of thunder. Seeing a giant outside the gates of Asgard was enough to make Thor send his hammer Mullicrusher soaring into the sky. It was he who paid the giant his wages, but not with the sun or moon. In fact, he even denied him the right to return to Jotunheim. With only a single blow of the hammer the giant's skull exploded into dust, and his headless body plunged down into Niflhel, far below the lowest world.
'I don't care much for giants,' said Thor.
'That's pretty obvious,' said Heimdall.

But beautiful Freya could only wring her hands. She was very soft hearted and did not like violence. No-one knows what her feelings might have been if she had realized how the gods had nearly bartered her away into Jotunheim. The Æsir thought it best not to mention it.

As for Loki, he came back to Asgard the next day and he too looked exhausted. Some months later he gave birth to a foal: it was a grey and had eight legs. Odin took possession of him and called him Sleipnir. And that horse has always been the best among gods or in the world of men.

The apples of eternal life

When things were quiet in Asgard, Odin and the other gods sometimes wandered through the worlds to see how matters were arranging themselves. Quite often they did this in disguise: people were apt to become uneasy if they suspected any of the Æsir were among them. One bright morning Odin, with Loki and Hoenir, set out from Asgard on foot and tramped northwards over the mountains not noticing that the further they went the more desert-like the landscape became. There were no dwellings to be seen and that meant no supper.

In those days, when homes were few and far between, every householder felt it his duty to welcome strangers and to give them something to eat and a bed for the night. Odin told Hoenir and Loki to keep a sharp lookout for any sign of cottage smoke. They trudged on all day and did not see any. That night they had to wrap up in their woollen cloaks and go to sleep hungry on the ground.

Next day, they pressed on again and though the look of the countryside improved they saw no sign of life and were hard put to it to know where to find food and drink. Towards midday, when their hollow insides were beginning to rumble, they dropped down into a fertile wooded valley where a herd of red cattle was grazing in a meadow by a stream. The three gods cornered a steer between them and having killed it and skinned it soon set about roasting it on poles with a crossbar spit which they made from branches lying about.

When the ox looked as though it ought to be done and their mouths were already drooling at the thought of great juicy slices of beef, they sharpened their knives on stones and kicked away the charred embers – only to find the meat still raw and quite uncooked.

Patiently, they built the fire up once more and waited for another hour before scattering the glowing wood again. The meat was still not done, being colder and rawer than before in spite of having been twice at the centre of a roaring blaze.

Hoenir scratched his head. 'There's something funny going on here,' he muttered, poking at the meat hungrily with his knife.

Nearby stood a tall oak tree and they heard a voice coming from it, away above their heads. Odin turned sharply round.

'What's that? What do you say?' he cried angrily.

'The meat won't cook until I say so,' said the voice from the tree.

Odin, Loki and Hoenir left the failed ox-roast and stood looking up into the tree.

'Who are you, anyway?' demanded Odin.

Right at the top of the tree, on a very stout branch which nevertheless bent under his weight, a giant-sized eagle was perching. 'Never you mind,' said the eagle, 'the meat won't cook until I give the word.'

'Well, give the word then,' snapped Odin. 'Not until you agree to let me have my fill of the steer first,' said the eagle, 'then I'll allow it to cook through.'

Confronted with magic, and knowing no more powerful spell, there was nothing much the gods could do and since they were by now quite overpoweringly famished and tired they agreed to the conditions.

'Very well then,' said the eagle, 'start your fire and the meat will be done in just five minutes.'

So they began again. Just as the huge bird had indicated, the roast was cooked to a turn in five minutes. The eagle immediately flopped to the ground with a deafening flapping of its wings, sending a choking dust of ashes over them all. When they could see again, the greedy monster was scoffing up the precious meat in record-breaking time. Most of it had already disappeared into the eagle's stomach. As they rubbed their smarting eyes, they saw that all that was left hanging on the spit was the ox's skeleton.

Loki was always a good eater; now he licked away the useless saliva from his lips and clenched his fists wondering how to get his own back on the bird. Lying on the ground under the oak tree was a long bough which had broken off after a storm. Loki grabbed it with both hands and used it like a club, making a dead set at the eagle. The eagle sharply hopped a couple of jumps but the end of the pole hit him between the wings and stuck

there. As the eagle continued to hop, Loki was dragged off his feet and pulled along the ground. He tried to let go of the stick only to find he was unable to free himself; his fingers remained clutched round his end of the branch and nothing he could do would loosen them.

With great strides and a monstrous flapping of wings the eagle taxied off and Loki was pulled along unwillingly behind. Becoming airborne, the eagle flew just low enough for Loki's legs to bang painfully against the rocks. 'Stop it! Stop it!' he yelled, 'let me down!'

The flying eagle looked over his shoulder with his fierce eye and his huge curved beak terrified Loki still more but the bird said nothing.

Loki felt as though his arms would be torn out of his shoulders and he yelled hysterically at the top of his voice, begging the eagle to let him go. But the bird only flew higher and faster.

Soon the eagle reckoned that since his victim was sufficiently frightened the time was ripe to act and he said, 'I am the giant Thiazzi. Know this: I shall never let you loose – except perhaps at ten thousand metres – until you swear a solemn oath to deliver up the goddess Idunn to me. You must entice Idunn outside Asgard walls where I can get at her safely. And she must bring with her the casket of golden apples.'

By this time they were flying so high that Loki wondered in terror if they had not already reached ten thousand metres. Far below on the ground Odin and Hoenir were mere specks and the herd of cattle a group of red dots.

'Anything, anything! I'll swear to anything!' gasped Loki.

'It'll be the worse for you if you don't keep your oath!' croaked Thiazzi and to frighten Loki still further, he dropped out of the sky like a stone with such a plummeting rush that Loki's heart rose into his mouth. Then at a man's height from the ground, Thiazzi released him and Loki fell in a heap with a thump.

Massaging his painful arms and rubbing his

'You know they understand every word I say,' she told Loki. 'I praise them and it helps them to grow better.' Of course, it was well known that there was a special feeling between the goddess of Spring and flowers: as she walked in the fields she left behind her not footprints but flowers and their perfume stayed with her always.

'It's a lovely afternoon for a stroll,' said Loki. 'Do you know, I was in the woods just beyond Asgard walls the other day and I saw a fruit tree, quite out of the ordinary – well, I thought it extraordinary because it bore fruit like your golden apples.'

'Oh, I hardly think that could be possible,' said sweet Idunn because she knew her apples were unique.

'Would you like to come and see?' asked Loki, 'And perhaps you would care to bring your casket of apples so that we can compare the two. It would please Odin to know where there was a fresh source of supply.'

Loki's smooth talk completely deceived the innocent Idunn. She fetched her ashwood casket containing the apples of youth and together with Loki passed out through Asgard walls. The only person to see them go was Heimdall the Watchman. He nodded good afternoon but most of his attention was focused on an eagle wheeling far up in the sky over towards Jotunheim.

When Loki and Idunn were hidden from Asgard walls by a corner of the wood, the giant Thiazzi flew down in his eagle disguise and before Idunn knew what was happening his gnarled talons had gripped her by the shoulders and she and the apples were being whisked away through the air to Jotunheim.

Loki slyly crept back into Asgard making sure nobody saw him.

The Æsir were very upset by Idunn's disappearance and without their daily diet of the apples of youth they quickly began to grow old. With beards growing grey and bowed shoulders they hardly recognized each other. They started to shuffle about and peer short-sightedly. Their clothes hung off their backs. 'Where's Idunn, where is she?' they piped querulously. 'Something's got to be done!

shoulders and feeling very sorry for himself, Loki hobbled back to join his comrades. He made some excuses but told them nothing of what had really passed between him and the bird. They were none of them very happy about their encounter and decided at once to turn round and go back to Asgard.

The mischief maker of the gods was put into very low spirits by the trouble he had got himself into. He grew even more melancholy when he considered what the consequences would be when the Æsir lost Idunn's golden apples of youth and the fruit came into the possession of the giants. He worried and wondered over what he should do but could find no solution. He would have to keep his oath and deliver up Idunn; and without her enchanted apples to eat, the Æsir would lose their eternal youth and begin to grow old and grey. Old age, wrinkled faces, bowed backs, tottery legs, feebleness. He shuddered at the thought.

Loki went to find Idunn. She was walking about her garden talking to the flowers.

Who saw her last? Yes, who saw her last?'

It turned out that Heimdall was the last to have seen her walking from Asgard accompanied by Loki.

'Might have known it! Might have guessed it!' muttered Odin testily. 'Fetch him to me!' Loki was frog-marched into the presence of the Father of the Æsir and before long had given the whole story away. In their fury, the gods threatened the Mischief Maker with torture and death, and when he was sufficiently terrified, Loki declared he would go himself to Jotunheim and try to bring Idunn and her golden apples home. He made one request, that the goddess Freya should lend him her feather coat so that he could fly through the air disguised as a hawk. Freya, who by now was beginning to have wrinkles round her beautiful eyes, was only too willing. Loki put the hawk skin on and leaped into the air, flew over Asgard walls and with swift strokes of his wings headed out across the ocean to Jotunheim.

As it happened, the time he had chosen was a good one, for the giant Thiazzi had rowed out to sea to fish. With his sharp hawk's eye Loki swept the glittering water and saw Thiazzi far below dozing over his rod. As his glance flicked forward to the land he made out a bright glow moving along the battlements of the giant's castle. That could only be Idunn. The hawk stooped from the sky faster than light and landed on an embrasure where Idunn leaned to gaze longingly across the sea to where the bright towers of Asgard pierced the clouds. She gave a startled scream as the hawk perched by her and nearly dropped her ashwood casket of apples.

'Hist! It's me, Loki,' whispered the bird.

Thiazzi's daughter Skadi had come down from her mountain home in order to keep watch on Idunn but fortunately she had gone for a stroll around to the other side of the battlements and was hidden from view.

'Listen quickly Idunn!' said Loki, 'I am going to change you and your apples into a nut! I shall grip you in that form and carry you back to Asgard! Don't be afraid!'

This was no sooner said than done, and

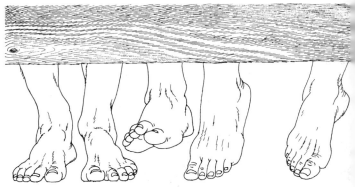

with the nut in his claws Loki dived upwards into the sky and struck out for home. At the moment of transformation, Skadi walked back onto the battlements. She was a clever girl and realized that by some magic means her prisoner was being spirited away. She could see her father a couple of miles off shore and she unwound her long white veil and waved it frantically to catch his attention. It was some time before Thiazzi jerked out of his daydream. Seeing the veil billowing backwards and forwards, he realized something was wrong and immediately flung his rod into the bottom of the boat with the line still trailing behind and rowed to the shore like a madman.

Skadi shouted down from the walls to her father. She pointed to a speck in the sky halfway across the ocean to Asgard.
'A hawk came and took away Idunn!' she cried. Thiazzi rushed into the castle looking for the peg where he had last hung his eagle coat.

At his post in Asgard, Heimdall saw in the distance a hawk in panic-stricken flight darting towards the walls and not far behind him a giant eagle. The Watchman raised the alarm and the gods crowded along the ramparts. The hawk was straining every feather, but Freya who owned the magic bird skin knew there was a limit to its speed.
'Thiazzi's eagle coat is bigger and faster than my hawk skin!' she cried and she wrung her lovely hands. 'Thiazzi is bound to overtake Loki!'

Tyr was the one who kept his head.
'Come on!' he shouted, 'get a whole heap of wood shavings! Frey! Balder! Help me!' Between them the young gods gathered bins of shavings from the carpenter's shop and

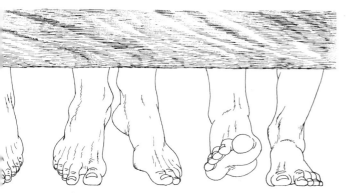

made a huge pile just outside Asgard walls.

The hawk was only half a mile away and the eagle not far behind him, already bringing his talons forward in expectation of the strike he would make before long. The walls of Asgard were the finishing line for this vital race and no-one could be certain whether the hawk or the eagle would win. Outside, below the walls the Æsir waited holding their breath. Tyr had a lighted torch in his hand.

The hawk got there first. With a whir of wings he sped over the upturned heads and into Asgard; down zoomed the eagle after him. Just before the giant bird reached the air above the shavings Tyr plunged his torch into the pile and a geyser of flame shot into the sky. It ran like wildfire through the eagle's plumes and Thiazzi's feather coat melted off him in a stinking cloud of smoke. The giant plunged down and forward against the walls of Asgard with a thud so tremendous it dented the stones inwards to form the shape of a man. Then the dead body tumbled into the roaring bonfire and was entirely consumed – except for the eyes which were hard as diamonds.

The gods hurried back into Asgard to see if Idunn and Loki were safe and sound. Loki was standing there trembling, his body drenched in sweat. Thankfully they saw that Idunn was also there, restored again to her beautiful self with her casket of apples held firmly in her hand. The gods and goddesses began munching at once and before supper-time they were all young again.

Their anger against Loki had not died down. They had had too narrow an escape for that. Some of them still wanted to do away with him, but Loki appealed to Odin and reminded him of their bond of blood-brotherhood. They were still arguing when a cry came from Heimdall the Watchman that a new enemy was at the gates.

Once more the gods and goddesses crowded to the battlements to confront the new danger. It was Skadi the daughter of Thiazzi dressed in full armour, and she demanded compensation for the death of her father.

The Æsir reminded her of how the dispute had started and said that her father must bear some of the blame for having played a trick on Odin, Hoenir and Loki with the steer which wouldn't cook. Nevertheless, they were willing to be reconciled with Skadi and to offer her compensation.

Skadi asked, 'What can compensate for a dead father?'

Loki said, 'Perhaps a live husband.'

The gods were shocked when Skadi appeared interested and enquired, 'Do you mean one of the Æsir?' Once again Loki was getting them into trouble.

'I will accept your offer,' said Skadi.

None of the Æsir wanted to marry Skadi, yet Odin said it must be done, so they came to a compromise. Skadi should be allowed to choose one of the gods but she would not know who it was she was selecting. She was to pick the one she wanted for a husband by looking at his feet.

So a screen was erected and the bashful Æsir who were eligible paraded behind it in bare feet. Skadi showed no hesitation. She knew who she wanted – Balder, the most beautiful of the gods. She saw one pair of feet and ankles surpassingly clean and fair. 'I choose this one,' she cried, 'there can be little about Balder that is ugly.' Unfortunately the clean feet belonged to Niord, god of the sea, who spent much of his time walking in the waves. And that is how this apparently ill-matched pair, one from the mountains, one from the sea, came to be married.

They do say also that later on Odin (or possibly Thor) compensated Skadi still further by taking her father Thiazzi's eyes and flinging them into the night sky to become twin stars – the same which today are called by his name in the northern lands.

Odin prepares for the Ragnarok

The loss of Idunn, although only for a short time, came as a great shock to the Æsir. They suddenly understood that her kidnapping might very well have been permanent. Their carefree innocent life in Asgard was ended and they had to keep a constant lookout for further attacks by their enemies the giants. Odin knew the perils in store better than the other gods because he could see into the future. He decided not only to take safety measures for the present but also to prepare actively for the evils that were to come.

First, he planned to keep the mountain and frost giants at bay by getting the burly thunder god Thor to attack them at frequent intervals – and always when they least expected it. Nothing pleased the rollicking, red-bearded, red-haired charioteer more. He was always delighted to be off in the east 'huntin' trolls', as he called it.

Next, Odin began to train his worshippers on Midgard so that when the time came for them to die they could join him in Asgard and swell his big battalions for the final battle. In times of peace, when Odin was sitting among his family and friends, his bearded face was so dignified and beautiful that everyone felt their spirits lifted up by a single glance from him. But in battle he appeared dreadful to his enemies and his glance had quite a different effect: by a mere look he could bring about what men on Midgard called 'the war-fetter'. On the battlefield he could turn his enemies blind and deaf and literally paralyse them with terror.

His own followers, on the other hand, were filled with eagerness to charge into the fight, snarling madly like dogs or wolves, becoming as strong as bears or wild bulls and savagely biting at their shield-rims. Such a fearful spectacle was often enough to make their enemies turn and flee. Their savage, inhuman behaviour was called 'running berserk', and they themselves were named 'berserks'.

The berserks used to black their shields, paint their bodies black and choose the very darkest nights for their battles. Only the whites of their eyes gleamed in the blackness and their frightened opponents believed them to be devils. Some wore iron rings rivetted round their necks, never taking them off (it needed the services of a blacksmith to remove them) until they had killed a man. Because they wore wolfskins and bearskins some people say they actually became werwolves, turning from men into wolves in times of danger. Others believe that the skins gave them their name, for berserk means 'bear sark' or bear shirt.

In time, berserks like these were to be found in the bodyguards of the kings of many of the northern lands. Most northern kings claimed Odin as their ancestor and to be a berserk in their service was regarded as a training for life after death in Asgard when berserks would act as Odin's own henchmen.

King Gylfi had himself been a bodyguard to a king, though he was not a berserk. He had fought alongside the famous Viking king Olaf Tryggvason at the battle of Maldon in England. What he now learned about the berserks reminded him that many of the young men fighting beside him seemed actually to have enjoyed the experience. The smell of blood and sour sweat seemed to intoxicate them, doubling their physical strength and daring. Their nostrils flared, they pawed the ground and their fingers on axe handles and sword hilts sweated and itched to come to blows. They were quite certain that death in battle was the direct route to Asgard.

A voice broke into King Gylfi's daydream. 'You don't appear to be listening very attentively,' said High, while Just-as-High and the Third frowned disapprovingly. 'Have you heard enough?'
'No, no, your worships,' said Gylfi quickly. 'You were telling me about the warriors of Asgard.'

As well as training warriors on Midgard, Odin formed an army of women in Asgard, the Valkyries or Odin's Maids. The Valkyries had a special responsibility. Odin used to send these warrior women, splendidly armed and riding spirited flying horses, to battlefields on Midgard. There they chose those who died a valiant death to come and join Odin in Asgard.

The Valkyries wore shining mailcoats and helmets and carried all kinds of weapons including swords, spears, battle-axes and shields. However, they did not take part in the actual fighting and were not supposed to interfere by influencing who was to win and who was to be killed. They simply carried out Odin's orders. If they disobeyed (and sometimes this did happen) then they had to face Odin's terrible wrath.
'Indeed,' said Gylfi, 'I have heard of men who dreamed of terrible witch-women before a battle, waiting to rake up the dead. Perhaps these were really Valkyries.'
'War is a grisly business, brutal, wasteful and best avoided,' replied High. 'Few, if any who are engaged in it escape being brutalized themselves. But for those who die bravely, there is a new life ahead in Valhalla, the Hall of the Slain.
'Valhalla is a huge fortress, shining bright with gold. It has high walls stretching far and wide in that region of Asgard called Gladsheim. The rafters supporting the roofs are mighty spears, the tiles are colossal shields and the benches in the vast hall itself are strewn with war coats. Over the western door is fixed a gigantic wolf's head and an eagle tirelessly wheels above. Perched on Valhalla's highest roof-ridge like a living weathercock stands Gullinkambi, the cock who will crow just once, to awaken the warriors when the morning of Ragnarok dawns.'
'What an eye-staggering building Valhalla must be!' said Gylfi. 'And yet I suppose there are quite often queues and double-queues before its doors, considering the number of wars human-beings fight and the multitudes of men slaughtered in Midgard's battles.'

High replied tartly, 'Why don't you ask a plain question if you want to know how many doors there are in Valhalla and how big they are? However many people die in battle, you can be certain that anyone who has earned a place there will find it: there is free entry and a seat at table for them all. Through its doors the host of warriors enter and through

them they will race to arms at the last roll call before Ragnarok. For these are the Einheriar, the Chosen Champions of Odin.'
'But what do they do all the time?' asked Gylfi. 'I don't suppose such brave warriors are content with just eating and drinking all day long.'

High answered, 'Every morning as soon as they are dressed they put on their mailcoats and helmets, file in an orderly fashion, left-right, left-right, onto the battlefield, fight and kill one another. That is their sport. Sometimes one gets killed, sometimes another. It's impossible to tell from day to day who will win and who will lose and it doesn't matter how much blood flows or how great the slaughter is: as soon as daylight fails the battle stops. Then the real magic is seen. All the blood dries up and disappears; heads, arms and legs which have been chopped off rejoin their bodies; the dead come alive and scramble to their feet as the bugler blows the "fall in".

'The armies then march back to Valhalla and spend the evening and far into the night eating, drinking and telling tales of the day's fighting. The Valkyries who brought them to Asgard now wait on them in Valhalla, carrying round the drinks, keeping the horns brim full and the tables replenished with food.'
'Ah yes,' remarked Gylfi. 'You tell me every-one who has ever fallen in battle from the beginning of the world comes to Odin in Valhalla. How *does* he manage to supply them all with food and drink?'
'It is true that there are countless hosts, great armies of champions in Valhalla. And there will be millions more to come unless there's a radical change in men's behaviour – which I don't expect. But still there can never be so great a multitude in Valhalla that the meat of their enchanted boar Sæhrimnir will ever once fail to feed them all. That pig has a charmed life – and death. Every single day he is butchered, cooked and eaten. And every night he springs to life again ready for the next day's feasting! We believe he even enjoys it himself, for he never fails to provide such juicy pork, such savoury crackling. The

cook's stewpot is just as magical as the pig, for it never becomes empty until the last man has been served.'
'What do the Champions have to drink which can possibly slake their thirst and satisfy them as the meat satisfies their hunger – or is water the only drink there?'

High replied: 'Now isn't that a silly question for a grown man to ask?' He glanced at Just-as-High and the Third. 'He wants to know if the Father of All, having ceremoniously invited kings, jarls and other proud nobles into his home, will offer them – water! I'll wager many of the warriors would feel they had paid a high price for their drink of water if they got no better entertainment – the men who work their passage to death through blood and fire! WATER!' he shouted, 'far from it. A gigantic she-goat

called Sky-Leaper supplies all the drink they need. She stands on her hind legs in Valhalla, stretching up to nibble the needles of a great pine tree. Now that goat does not give milk, as a simpleton like you might think. She gives a far more potent liquid – mead! It squirts of its own accord so copiously from her two teats that every day she fills an enormous vat: quite big enough, anyway, to make all the Champions roaring drunk after their daily battle.'

'No wonder warriors on Midgard hold earthly life so cheap and are so eager to die and be carried to Valhalla,' said Gylfi.

'Fighting without death; eating and drinking as much as they please. It sounds a very pleasant way to live. Surely all these fine fighters will be strong enough to win at the Ragnarok.'

'You forget,' said High. 'Those down in the Underworld are also making their counter plans. Remember the terrifying dragon-ship they are building. That ship is frightening to everyone on the side of the Æsir for two reasons: first because of the horrid materials from which she is being carpentered – the parings of dead men's nails. And secondly because of her monstrous size. That ship will be big enough to carry all the dead who have gone down to Hel since the beginning of time. All the murderers, adulterers and oath-breakers will crowd aboard her. I will not tell you now who her helmsman will be, because you would hardly believe me. It is enough for you to know that he will be one of the most evil and dangerous of the gods' enemies, a mischievous and mighty captain. You already know the ship's name, of course – it is Naglfar.'

'But isn't Odin also making certain there are trained leaders on Midgard who will be able to help him marshall his men at the last battle?' asked Gylfi.

'Certainly,' said High. 'He pays frequent visits to Midgard in disguise, mainly to choose his generals. Most die a hero's death in battle, but sometimes they come to him as sacrifices, by hanging. To die as a sacrifice is no disgrace: remember Odin himself

hung for nine days and nights on the Tree. But not everyone wants to die that way. And some, as you will see, even try to get the benefits of sacrifice without paying the price.'

Gylfi, realizing he was about to hear another story, did not interrupt again.

There was once a famous Viking leader, King Vikar, who was becalmed with his longship on a foreign shore. After waiting for many days, the king decided to pray to Odin for a favourable wind and to offer one of the crew of Vikings as a sacrifice to strengthen his prayer. The crew wanted the victim to be chosen by lot and King Vikar insisted that he himself should take part in the draw. When the lots were drawn, everybody

was appalled to see that King Vikar
was to be the victim.

The men did not want to see their king
hanged, even as a sacrifice to Odin, so after
arguing among themselves for a time, someone
suggested they make a mock sacrifice
instead of a real one.

Next day, King Vikar was made to stand
on a tree stump with a calf's intestines strung
loosely round his neck in place of a rope.
The other end of the gut was placed over the
bough of a fir tree. Starkad, one of the crew,
took his place beside the king, intending to
poke him gently with a stick as he uttered
the ritual words: 'Now I give thee to Odin.'

As Starkad said the words, the stick he

was holding turned into a sharp spear and his
gentle poke stabbed far into the king's
chest; at the same time the calf's soft intestines
became a strong cord and the fir bough
bent upwards, lifting King Vikar's body high
into the tree. Wounded by the spear and
strangled by the cord, he quickly died
in the branches.

'Which only goes to show,' said High 'that
even kings should be careful not to mock
Odin. He is stern but he is just. It's best for
you men of Midgard to be prepared to meet
him at any time.

'Now if you stop looking so apprehensive
I'll tell you about the adventures of some of
Odin's chosen heroes on Midgard.'

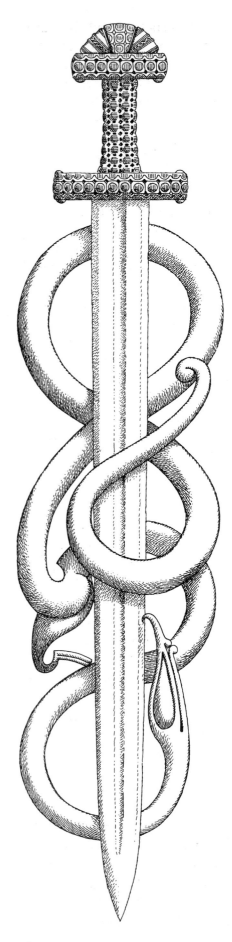

Sigurd the dragon-slayer

The three gods Odin, Hoenir and Loki had been walking about Midgard for some time when at last they came to a marshy and wooded part of Denmark. Through the trees they could hear the noise of splashing water and because they were tired and thirsty, they followed a path towards the sound and came upon a waterfall dropping into a dark tarn. Lying asleep at the edge of the pool was an otter as big as a man. The gods were hungry as well as thirsty and Loki quickly grabbed a huge pebble, flung it at the slumbering otter and killed it. Within minutes the three gods had skinned it, spitted the carcass, roasted and eaten it.

Fed and watered, they began to look about for shelter for the night and not far from the pool they discovered a house. Loki went up to the door carrying the otter skin over his left arm thinking that, if the worst came to the worst, he could barter it for a night's lodging. The house belonged to a man called Kreidmar and as soon as he lifted the latch and saw the otter skin he shouted over his shoulder for his thralls to run quickly and bind the three strangers.

'What's all this about?' cried the struggling Loki. 'Don't you know the laws of hospitality? You're expected to give at least one night's lodging to any chance passers-by.'

'Not when those passers-by have just murdered my son,' growled Kreidmar.

It turned out that Kreidmar's son Otter was a shape-shifter who used to assume the form of an otter to hunt in the tarn for salmon. He had just caught and eaten one and was sleeping off the meal when Loki had killed him.

Loki said to Kreidmar in his most ingratiating way, 'My good sir: you must understand that we are strangers here and if not completely innocent, at least nearly so. How were we to know that your excellent son was in the habit of masquerading as an otter? We are all three extremely sorry and I am sure that if there is anything, anything at all we can do to repay you for your loss, we will not hesitate for a moment.'

Kreidmar looked at them calculatingly. 'Only one thing will

ransom my dead son,' he said. 'You must fill
his otter skin with gold and then cover
the gold-stuffed skin with still more gold until
nothing of the pelt can be seen.'
'We'll do it, sir, we'll do it,' cried Loki.
'But how, prisoners as we are, can we get any
gold?'

Kreidmar said, 'In that waterfall by the pool
lives the dwarf Andvari, in the shape
of a sharp-toothed pike. He guards a fabulous
treasure – you may have caught sight of it
gleaming there when you were killing my son!
Get me that treasure. It will stuff and cover
my son's skin.'
'But that pike is no common creature,' said
Loki. 'No ordinary rod and line will bring him
to land.'
'That is true,' said Kriedmar. 'The only way
to catch Andvari is with the magic net of Ran
the sea-ogress. Loki, you shall try.'

So Loki was freed and went at once to
borrow Ran's magic net. He returned quickly
to Andvari's pool. Down, deep down in
the depths of the water he could see twinkles
of golden light with a dark shadow passing
back and forth: it was Andvari the dwarf in
his shape of a pike.

Andvari saw the openwork pattern
hovering just over his treasure and he flicked
his tail to propel himself towards it.
He thought it must be a reflection of the twigs
from the trees overhanging the pool, but
with such a treasure to guard, it was as well
to inspect every changing light and shadow.
As soon as he was in the centre of the
circle Loki snatched on the cord and Andvari
the pike was caught.

By the time Loki had landed his struggling
catch, Andvari was thoroughly frightened:
with his round fish's eyes he gazed up and saw
Loki about to smash a weighty pebble
on his head. 'Stop! Stop!' shouted Andvari,
shifting himself back into his dwarf's shape,
for a fish can breathe only a very short time
out of water. 'What can I do to save
my life?' 'Give me your treasure!' said Loki.

No matter how Andvari argued,
Loki would not agree to any other terms and
eventually the dwarf agreed to give up

his gold. He uttered a spell and all the water
drained suddenly from the pool, leaving the
treasure shining in the sunlight. There
were heaps and heaps of gold brooches, neck
torques, ornaments and rings. One ring in
particular Andvari tried to conceal. But Loki
had seen it.
'Do not force me to give you this ring,'
warned Andvari quietly. 'There is a curse on
it. Whoever owns it once it leaves my
possession will suffer terrible disaster.'
'Stuff and nonsense,' said Loki and pocketed
the ring. Then he forced the dwarf to help
him carry the treasure to Kreidmar's house.

Odin and Hoenir were freed to help with
the next task and the skin was stuffed and
covered. But Kreidmar said with a cruel grin:
'Look! There at the muzzle! I can see one
whisker still uncovered. You have all failed.
I shall kill you!'

Loki rubbed his smooth chin and glanced
at Kreidmar. His fingers rubbed the ring
in his pocket. 'I have one more gold ring,' he
muttered to Kreidmar, 'but I warn you
not to take it. There is a powerful curse on it,
and if you become its owner, disaster is sure
to follow!'

Kreidmar laughed. 'Give me the ring at
once. It will just cover the whisker and then
you can all go!' He snatched the ring from
Loki's reluctant hand. 'Be off!' he said. 'And
think yourselves lucky!'

But Kreidmar had been foolish to disregard
the curse, which soon began to take effect.
Kreidmar had two other sons in addition to
Otter, one called Fafnir (another shape-shifter)
and one called Regin. Regin was the
most skilful smith in Denmark, having been
trained by the dwarfs in their underground
smithies. He was away working with the
dwarfs, but Fafnir was living at home.

The thought of the treasure haunted Fafnir
day and night and before long he made
up his mind to take it away from Kreidmar.
Obviously Kreidmar was not going to part
with it willingly, and Fafnir knew he would
have to murder his father for the gold. His
avarice grew day by day until one dark night
the vision of gold before his eyes blotted out

all other thoughts and Kreidmar was killed.

Nothing but greed and spite now filled Fafnir's thoughts. All he wanted to do was to hide the gold in some secret spot and lie and gloat over it. He removed the treasure by night to a rocky cave and there he changed himself into a monstrous dragon which lay, coil upon coil, breathing fire and smoke and guarding his golden treasure.

Some years before these events a young man, Sigmund, lived with his father King Volsung. One day a wedding feast was being held for his twin sister, Signy, who was to marry the King of Gothland, a man named Siggeir.

The hall of the Volsungs where the wedding feast was held had a very strange feature: it had been built round a massive living oak tree whose trunk supported the roof and whose leafy branches overspread the whole of the building. The oak tree was known far and wide as the Branstock.

Half way through the feast, a stranger entered. He wore a wide-brimmed slouch hat, a travel-stained cloak and linen trousers. His feet were bare and he had only one eye.

Contrasting oddly with the stranger's poor appearance was a marvellous naked sword which he gripped in his right hand. Without a word he walked straight up to the Branstock and plunged the blade into the tree as far as the hilt.

'Whoever draws this sword from the tree may keep it as a gift from me,' he announced. 'In the whole wide world there is none better. Its blade will never fail until I call its rightful possessor to me.' And he strode out again into the night.

There was a sudden buzz of excited talk. Every Viking present tried to pull out the sword. One after another, tugging and grunting, their brawny muscles rippling from wrist to shoulder, their eyes bulging in the torchlight, they failed to move it by so much as a hair's breadth. King Volsung himself failed; the bridegroom King Siggeir failed; all King Volsung's nine sons failed – until it came to the youngest, Signy's twin brother Sigmund. The handsome, golden-haired boy laid his hands on the jewelled hilt and the sword almost pushed him backwards as it slid easily out of the tree.

Sigmund's sword served him well, though it led to bitter quarrels and fighting. Many years later Sigmund, now the last of the famous Volsung line, lay dying on the battlefield. His wife, Hiordis, stole out at night from her hiding place to search for her husband among the dead and wounded. At last she found him. Seeing that he was near to death she began to pray.

'Save your prayers, for I shall not recover from these wounds,' whispered Sigmund, his voice anxious and urgent. 'Listen carefully to what I have to say. It is important that I tell you quickly about the sword.

'You know that King Siggeir treacherously murdered my father and my nine brothers and gained possession of the sword. After years of struggle I myself avenged my family and killed Siggeir to regain the sword. It has won every battle for me until now. Listen carefully: in the middle of this battle, when everything was going our way, a stranger walked onto the battlefield and came straight towards me. He was wearing a black cloak, a slouch hat – and he had only one eye. In his hands he carried a mighty spear, greater than any spear I have ever seen. I struck the shaft of the spear with my sword and the blade shattered into three pieces. I knew then who the stranger was and that he had come himself to summon me to Valhalla.'

Sigmund's wounds began to smart with the cold and he feared that he would die before he had time to finish. 'Now my dear queen and wife, you must leave me. But you must take the pieces of the sword – here they are – and escape. You are carrying within you our son who, when he is born and grows up will be a far more famous warrior than I have been. Then the sword will be forged again and become the greatest weapon the world has ever known.'

Hiordis escaped from the battle in a small open boat and, after drifting helplessly at sea, was cast ashore on the coast of Denmark, the country where the dragon Fafnir still

guarded his glittering, golden hoard.

In those days the king of Denmark was called Jalprek. His son, Alf, fell in love with Hiordis and after a while they were married. Soon after the wedding Hiordis gave birth to a boy and named him Sigurd.

In those days it was usual for lads, even high-born ones, to learn a useful trade and Alf put Sigurd to smithying. The smith he chose as tutor was none other than Regin, the son of Kreidmar and brother of Fafnir.

Regin was no ordinary blacksmith; he had learned his trade among the dwarfs and they had also taught him the secret of the magic runes. He was a wise, learned man and he taught Sigurd many things but he was also something of a troublemaker. One day he said to Sigurd: 'I wish they wouldn't treat you as if you were a scullion here. You must agree that they make you feel a bit like a poor relation.'

Sigurd had grown into a fine, honest young man. 'You are mistaken,' he said. 'My step-father Alf will give me anything I want.' 'Then ask him to give you a horse,' said Regin.

Sigurd did as Regin had suggested and Alf told him to go to the woods where the horses were running wild and help himself. On his way to the forest, Sigurd met an old, long-bearded stranger who asked, 'Where might you be hurrying off to, young man?' 'I'm going to choose a horse,' said Sigurd. 'Perhaps you would like to help me.' 'Certainly,' said the stranger. Between them they drove a herd of horses out of the trees.

The stranger suggested they should make the horses swim in the nearby river as a test. All the animals swam easily across and all except one galloped off on the other side. The one that came back was a fine grey stallion with a proudly arched neck and fierce, keen eyes. The stranger said, 'You can take my word for it, this is the best horse in the world. He is a descendant of Odin's own eight-legged Sleipnir. He will carry you swiftly and safely in war and peace.'

The stranger disappeared as mysteriously as he had come, before Sigurd had time to thank him properly.

'I wonder,' said Sigurd to himself. 'They say that Odin visits the world of men in disguise to prepare his warriors. Perhaps, just perhaps, he is thinking of me.' He patted the grey stallion thoughtfully. 'A descendant of Sleipnir will be a horse indeed,' he said. 'I'll call you Grani.'

As Regin watched Sigurd learn and become more skilled, he decided to use him in a scheme which had long been hatching in his mind. This was no less a plot than to secure for himself the treasure which was still being guarded and gloated over by his brother, turned dragon, Fafnir.

When Regin first mentioned the idea to Sigurd, Sigurd was surprised. 'I think it is a stirring idea to fight a dragon and win back the treasure – but why do you want me to do it? I'm only a boy still. I have a good horse, I know, but I don't even have a man's sword yet, let alone one that would stand up against his iron scales and the flames

which roar out from his fiery nostrils.'
Regin said, 'I myself will forge you a suitable
sword. All the skill of the dwarfs and the
magic of the runes will go into its forging.'

He went into his smithy, blew up the fire
and hammered out a blade. When it was
tempered and cool, he passed it to Sigurd.
Sigurd swung it above his head, two-handed,
and brought it down with a clash onto the
anvil. The blade broke into little pieces.

Regin went back to work and forged a
second sword. Again Sigurd tested it on the
anvil and again it shattered into small pieces.
A tiny misgiving entered Sigurd's mind.
Regin seemed just too eager for him to attack
Fafnir. He told his doubts to his mother.
'My son,' said Hiordis, 'just before your
father King Sigmund died, he gave me the
pieces of his incomparable sword – the sword
drawn from the Branstock all those
years ago. He told me to give them to you
to be forged again into a blade which would
never fail. Here they are. Take them to
Regin. He will make you a sword which you
will call Gram, the King, for it will be the
king of swords. With Gram in your hands you
need not be afraid of any of Regin's
schemes.'

Once more Regin worked the bellows to
blow the fire of his forge to a white heat.
When the pieces of Sigmund's sword shone in
the furnace like incandescent ice, Regin
drew them out and found that they ran
together of their own accord on the anvil. He
thrust the blade back into the furnace
and when he pulled it out of the coals for the
last time and plunged it into the hissing
water-tank, to temper it, blue fire seemed still
to burn along its edges. He gave the
smoking weapon to Sigurd who raised it high
above his head in his right hand, to
bring its keen, delicate sharpness against the
blunt head of the iron anvil.

The sword sliced the anvil in two.

With his horse Grani and his new sword
Gram Sigurd was now ready to ride out alone
to do battle against the dragon. But
Regin insisted on going with him to act as
his guide to the dragon's lair.

Regin knew the way well and they made
good progress. After three days they came to
a desolate heath. Here and there ancient
rocks twisted from the black earth like broken
bones and once or twice they had to pick
their way through dark, sinister woods.
Swamp and marsh sent poisonous fumes into
the stagnant air, and when darkness fell,
they could see eerie lights floating about the
wrinkled surface of the fen. They spent
the night uncomfortably by bushes hung with
water-drops. In the grey dawn they trod
an upward path leading their horses to edge a
way round windy cliffs, using wolf-trails
until all tracks finished. Before them lay a
black tarn surrounded by high rocky cliffs.
'This pool is Fafnir's water-hole,' said Regin.
'On that cliff over there, you will find a
track worn by his body as he crawls from his
cavern in the middle of the morning to slake
his thirst at the pool. His huge, snake-like
trunk hangs in coils over the rocks while his
jaws skim the water, his burning eyes ever
watchful, his head swaying backwards and
forwards. And fire shoots from his nostrils.
Look: you can see the rushes and reeds
at the edge of the water are scorched and
charred. Be careful. Watch that his blood
does not get on you. It will burn you up. I
dare come no further.'

Sigurd remounted Grani and rode on,
carefully skirting the shore of the gloomy lake.
Beside the cliff he came to a little wood
which he thought would hide his approach to
Fafnir's den.

Suddenly he was aware of a figure standing
in the shadows beneath a tree. It was an
old man with a long beard and only one eye
under his floppy-brimmed hat. He had
pulled his worn cloak round him to get some
protection against the dank, mist-laden air.
'Where are you riding, my son?' asked the
stranger.
'To do battle with Fafnir,' said Sigurd.
'Then take my advice,' said the one-eyed man,
'do not approach the dragon head-on.
If you do, his flames will burn you to a cinder
before you have a chance to strike
a blow at him with your sword.'

'What should I do, then?' asked Sigurd.

The stranger said, 'Dig a hole in the track worn by the dragon and wait there with Gram in your hand until you judge his heart is over your head. Then and only then, thrust Gram home with all your strength. One last thing. The blood of that dragon has magic properties. It will not burn you as Regin has said. When Fafnir is dead, strip naked and bathe in his blood. Wherever it touches you, you will be invulnerable; no weapon will harm you afterwards.' And the old man vanished.

This time, Sigurd was in no doubt about who the stranger was, and he did exactly as he had been advised. Soon he had dug a pit in the dragon's path and scrambled into it.

The first sign of Fafnir's approach was a distant rumbling: the ground began to tremble and then to shake; a whiff of sulphurous smoke drifted across the hole above him, followed by a swirl of flame. The edge of his pit crumbled as Fafnir's rattling scales scraped across it and the thick, snake-like body blotted out the daylight. Sigurd waited until he thought the beast's heart must be exactly above him. Then he thrust upwards, two-handed, with all his strength. The sword Gram pierced the iron scales; its point ran into Fafnir's evil heart.

As the waterfall of blood ran down Sigurd stripped off his clothing, letting it drench him from head to toe; only one tiny part of his body remained dry and that was where a sprig of heather, dislodged by Fafnir from the rocks, had drifted down and stuck between Sigurd's bare shoulders.

Sigurd used his sword to dig himself out of the pit and then saw Fafnir knotted and buckled in his death agony, his great tail still weakly swingeing, his jaws flat on the ground with dying wreaths of smoke rising from his nostrils.

Regin came puffing up. 'Brave lad!' he crowed, a covetous gleam in his eyes. 'We've done it. You've killed the dragon and at last the treasure is ours. There is one thing more I want you to do for me, though. You know that Fafnir was my brother. Yes,

he was evil, but I don't want his spirit to die entirely. Cut out his heart if you please and roast it. I myself will eat it and some of him will live on in me.'

Sigurd thought this a strange request but nevertheless he did as his old tutor had asked. He built a fire of twigs and as the heart was cooking on the end of a stick which Sigurd held over the flames, a little of the hot blood ran down and burned his finger. It stung so much that Sigurd dropped the stick and put his finger into his mouth.

No sooner had the blood touched his tongue than he heard strange voices coming from a bush nearby. There was no-one in sight and it was some seconds before Sigurd realized that he could understand the language of the birds. The first voice twittered, 'What a pity Sigurd is roasting the heart for someone else. He should eat it himself and become the wisest of men.'
'Yes, I know,' chirruped a second bird. 'Then he would understand that Regin intends to kill him and take all the treasure for himself.'
'If he had any sense he would strike Regin's head off with his sword,' replied the first bird. 'But look! I'm afraid it's too late.'

Sigurd glanced over his shoulder and saw Regin just about to strike him with a dagger. He sprang quickly to his feet and with a swift stroke of his sword took off Regin's head.

Then Sigurd mounted Grani and rode to the dragon's cave. He slid from the saddle and peered into the deep, dark hole. Gleaming like a lighted lamp on top of the heap of glittering treasure lay a golden ring, the ring that held Andvari's curse. Sigurd reached in, grasped the ring and put it in his pocket.

Sigurd was just about to lower himself into the cave to inspect the treasure more closely when he heard the birds' voices again.
'Sigurd should leave the gold where it is,' said one, 'and waste no time in riding to Hindfell to win the maiden who is worth more than any treasure.'
'True,' said another, 'I don't know why he is not half-way there already. His horse knows

the way. The treasure will be safe here.'

Sigurd climbed back into the saddle at once and Grani galloped off. Although night had fallen, Grani sped along, breathing evenly, snorting occasionally, yet moving always without hesitation, as though he was quite certain of his route. Soon Sigurd saw a glow in the sky. As he galloped nearer, he saw that the glow came from an extensive ring of fire encircling the mountain top, and within the ring stood a magnificent castle. 'On, Grani, on!' cried Sigurd. 'Leap this blazing barrier! Only you can do it!'

Grani felt Sigurd's knees grip his flanks and with a huge leap he cleared the magic burning circle and alighted unharmed in a marble-flagged courtyard.

Sigurd dismounted and let the reins hang. Before him was an open platform raised up three steps and flanked on all sides with slender pillars supporting rounded arches. In the centre of the space was a wonderfully ornamented bed and lying flat on the bed a fully armed warrior. The head was covered with a masked helmet and the body with a tight-fitting mailcoat, stretching from knees to shoulders. On the marble floor at the bed foot lay a shield and spear. The warrior, whoever he was, appeared to be dead and lying in state.

Sigurd climbed the steps and examined the splendid helmet-mask. Above the eye-holes were golden eyebrows inlaid with silver wire to represent hair; the golden moustache had inlaid silver wire for whiskers. With both hands, Sigurd gently lifted the helmet off the head. A cascade of yellow hair rippled free: the warrior was a beautiful young woman.

Sigurd saw that the figure was breathing, apparently not dead but under some spell. Gently he took his sword and drew its point from the neck of the mailcoat to the hem of its metal skirt. The armour split apart revealing a young woman dressed in white.

The young woman sat up and Sigurd sat facing her on the bed. She told him a strange story. Her name was Brynhild and she had been one of Odin's Valkyries. During a battle in which Odin had promised victory to

a great fighter called Helm Gunnar, Brynhild had disobeyed Odin's wishes and allowed Helm Gunnar's enemy to win. As a punishment, Odin had condemned her to marry the first mortal she met, no matter how old, crippled and cowardly he might be.

Brynhild had begged for mercy, but Odin would not change his mind. At last he had agreed to lay her sleeping on Hindfell behind a barrier of magic flames.
'I knew then that only a brave mortal would dare to burst through the enchanted wall. And if no mortal came, well, then, I would sleep for eternity.'

In his turn Sigurd told her his own story, how he was the son and grandson of a king; how he had slain a fearsome dragon and won a fabulous treasure. He even told her how the dragon's blood had made him invulnerable. 'Except, that is, for a spot between my shoulder-blades where a piece of heather fell. But who would strike a man there?' said Sigurd.

Then Sigurd took the fatal ring from his pocket and put it on Brynhild's finger to plight their troth.
'I swear by Odin's wrath that I will never love any man but you,' said Brynhild.
'I swear by my sword Gram, the gift of Odin himself, that my love for you will never die,' replied Sigurd solemnly. Then, vowing to return as soon as he had disposed of his treasure in a safe place, Sigurd mounted Grani and leaped back through the flames.

But Sigurd's adventures were not over yet. Andvari's curse quickly began to affect him. As soon as he had taken the treasure back to the Danish king's palace, his mother insisted that he must avenge his father Sigmund's death. Sadly, Sigurd recognized he had a sacred duty to perform.

After many months of bitter fighting, he and his Vikings slew the enemy king and Sigurd was able to return home. As he made his way back to Denmark he passed through the land of King Giuki, who ruled the region south of the river Rhine.

Giuki's queen was as scheming as she was beautiful. Her name was Grimhild and she

already head over heels in love with Sigurd and before very long the two were married.

Gudrun was a good and beautiful girl and the two were for a time very happy together. And so they would have continued if Gunnar, Sigurd's new brother-in-law, had not decided to go on a quest. He had heard of a maiden who lay under a spell, surrounded by a barrier of fire and he asked Sigurd to go with him to rescue her.

Sigurd rode with Gunnar and his two brothers Hogni and Guttorm to Hindfell, remembering nothing about his earlier visit, though his horse Grani pranced along eagerly, his ears twitching joyfully as they neared the mountain.

When they came to the magic flames, Gunnar set his horse at the barrier, but he was terrified and refused to jump. Gunnar asked Sigurd if he might borrow Grani but he, too, refused to carry Gunnar over the fire. 'Let me ride Grani through the flames,' suggested Sigurd. 'He will carry me. But first you had better change armour with me. I will take your shield and I will wear your helmet with the face-mask drawn down.'

This time Grani leaped easily over the barrier and Sigurd, fully armed, walked up to Brynhild. She was wearing the ring which had been their love-token but Sigurd had no recollection of it. He greeted her: 'I am Gunnar, son of King Giuki. I have ridden through the magic flames and I have come to take you away to be my bride.'

Brynhild was perplexed. She thought there was something about this proud, masked warrior she recognized and she asked him to remove his helmet. Sigurd said as politely as he could that this was not possible until they had ridden back through the fire. 'But it is night now,' said Brynhild, 'and I am too tired to make the attempt before morning. Look, the bed is large enough for both of us. Let us wait here until dawn.'

At first Sigurd refused to wait, but Brynhild would not go. So the pair went to the bed, Sigurd in all his armour, his masked helmet on his head. As they lay down,

and the king had three sons called Gunnar, Hogni and Guttorm and a daughter, Gudrun.

Queen Grimhild looked at Sigurd with her scheming green eyes. His golden-red hair fell to his shoulders and his neatly trimmed beard was the same colour; his nose was strong and high, like his cheekbones; his eyes were keen and intelligent and his shoulders were wide and strong. In fact he was in every way fit to marry her daughter. There was, however, something strange about his expression: it was as if he was looking inwards to another world. And sometimes a strange fire burned in his eyes, like a circle of magic flame.

Queen Grimhild took no chances. When Sigurd had been staying with them for some days she concocted a powerful love potion which she poured into his wine. At once he forgot all about Brynhild, whose image he had carried in his head through all the months of fighting, and instead fell in love with Grimhild's daughter Gudrun. Gudrun was he placed his naked sword between them, top to toe.

Next day Sigurd woke first and saw the gold ring on Brynhild's finger. Perhaps some distant memory came to him, perhaps it was just a moment of madness; for whatever reason, he gently slipped it off and put it in his pocket.

That morning, with Brynhild riding behind him, Sigurd jumped Grani out of the magic castle, and cantered up to the tents where the brothers were waiting. Sigurd dismounted and walked into Gunnar's tent and the pair changed back into their own armour. Then Gunnar ceremoniously removed his face-mask, claimed Brynhild for his bride and they all rode back to King Giuki's palace. Though Brynhild tried to speak to Sigurd he looked at her politely, like a stranger. Half convinced that their earlier meeting had been a dream, she abandoned the attempt. The next day, Gunnar and Brynhild were married.

With so many people involved in the deceit it was, perhaps, inevitable that Brynhild should find out the truth. It happened one day when Gudrun, Sigurd's wife, had walked to the river with Brynhild to bathe in a sheltered grassy inlet. By this time Gudrun had learned from her husband that he had impersonated Gunnar to rescue Brynhild. Gudrun had also begged and pleaded until Sigurd had reluctantly given her Brynhild's ring.

As the two women dared one another to go deeper and deeper into the water, they began to bicker.
'Afraid of a little water,' scoffed Gudrun. 'You are nothing but a coward.'
'Me a coward,' laughed Brynhild. 'Let me remind you that I am a Valkyr. I have ridden in the fiercest battles without fear. A little water will not frighten me.'
'Well in any case my husband is braver than yours,' said Gudrun childishly.
'That can hardly be true, either,' said Brynhild. 'No mortal but Gunnar would have dared to cross the magic flames to rescue me.'
'Nonsense!' cried the mortified Gudrun.
'Don't you know it was *my* husband Sigurd who leaped through the flames when Gunnar could not do it, not even on Grani. See, here is the ring he took from your finger to prove it. Now do you believe me?'

Brynhild was dumbfounded at this dreadful news. It seemed that not only had Sigurd betrayed their love; he had also made her break her oath to Odin that she would marry the mortal who rescued her from her enchanted prison. Her revenge was terrible. She told Gunnar she would not live with him as his wife unless he killed Sigurd. 'And there is only one place on his body where a sword can bite. He told me so himself. It is a spot between his shoulder-blades. Remember, I know his intimate secrets because he spent the night with me before he brought me through the flames to you!'

This, of course, made Gunnar very jealous but he was a good man and he could not bring himself to murder Sigurd. His brothers Hogni and Guttorm, however, were not so scrupulous and they secretly laid an ambush for Sigurd. While Guttorm attacked Sigurd from in front, Hogni stabbed him in the back between the shoulder-blades. So died Sigurd the dragon-slayer. The curse of Andvari's ring was fulfilled.

Gudrun ordered a great pyre to be built for her husband's funeral and Brynhild watched from the castle battlements as his body was borne shoulder high and the fire was set alight. As she saw Sigurd bathed in flames, she could no longer bear to be parted from him. She climbed a step to the ramparts and stood in an embrasure, her golden hair streaming in the wind. Flinging herself from the walls into the blazing pyre she cried: 'Sigurd, my beloved, wait for me! I too will brave the fire. Together we will rise to Odin in Valhalla!'

Not long after the pyre had burned itself out and nothing remained but a heap of grey ashes, one of the servants noticed that Grani, Sigurd's horse, was missing from his stall in the stables. Enquiries were made and a groom later admitted that he had seen the horse galloping into the sky. There were two riders, embracing, on his back.

The story of Trembling Hood

One dark and stormy night a young Viking was riding across a desolate moor in Denmark looking for the palace of King Rolf Kraki.

The name 'Kraki' is an odd one and you may wonder how he came by it. In those far-off days a man was named as the son of his father and because there were not all that many first names to go round, matters became a bit confusing. For instance, Olaf was a common name and soon in any town or village there would be a dozen 'Olaf son of Olafs' and nobody knew who was who. So it became the practice to give a man a nickname for something he had done or become famous for, or even just for his appearance. King Rolf was one of the tallest and thinnest of men and so people came to call him 'Kraki' which means 'Pole-Ladder'. A pole-ladder (which the Vikings used for scaling walls of towns they happened to be attacking) is a single pole with chocks on either side as steps, and nothing is much taller or thinner than that.

The young Viking who was riding over the moor that tempestuous night was called Biarki, but everybody knew him as Battle-Biarki because he was such a magnificent fighter. Like many strong men he could be very gentle and considerate, and that particular night he was anxious to find a shelter for his horse Hengist. But, baffled by the darkness and the mud, the horse lost the path and it seemed that the two would be swallowed up in the bog.

A clap of thunder startled Hengist and he shied. Battle-Biarki gentled him and said, 'Come up Hengist! There's nothing but noise in a thunder clap. Wait for the next lightning flash and then we'll make for that twisted thorn on higher ground I saw a minute back. Woa lad, woa! Wait, I'll cover you with my cloak over your haunches. Share and share alike . . . There lad.'

The horse nickered as though he understood every word. Biarki peered this way and that into the drenching black darkness. He could see nothing but dark even when he rubbed the rain, which was washing down his conical helmet, out of his eyes. The young warrior had almost come to the conclusion that it would be better to wait till dawn before moving: discomfort was much better than drowning in the marsh but suddenly he saw a pin prick of light.

'There's a cottage, Hengist!' he cried, 'and that means a bed for me and a dry stable for you! Tk, tk, come up lad.'

Battle-Biarki slipped out of the wet saddle and knocked on the door. There was some anxious whispering within. At last, 'Who's there?' asked a voice.

'Only a benighted traveller and his horse lucky enough to have escaped the bog.'

'What is your name good sir?'

'I'm called Biarki, though most men call me Battle-Biarki. Pray let us in. The storm still rages and we're wet and cold and hungry.' Slowly the door opened a little.

'Allow me to see your face, good sir, before I let the door off the chain. These are lawless times – well, well, come in.' An old man holding a lantern peered round the door post as the chain dropped free. 'But first, perhaps you would like to shelter your horse? Take this lantern. The stable is over there across the yard.'

The peasant's wife stood anxiously at his back and she asked timidly, 'Who is it, father?'

'Only a peaceful traveller caught by darkness on the moor. Don't fret mother.'

His wife asked, 'I wonder if he brings news of our son Hood?'

The old man said, 'Now why should he do that? He's a warrior – a splendid man even now bedraggled as he is with the pelting rain. He wears a helmet and a two-handled sword. And his cloak is rich enough though sodden by the storm. We've nothing to fear. His face is honest and his blue eyes twinkled in the lantern light. But of Hood? What would he know of Hood?'

'Poor Hood,' said the old woman, 'Oh, what's to become of him?'

'There, there mother!' said her husband, 'Don't you fuss. Hood will find his fortune one day. But now we must extend our hospitality to this stranger.'

As they were eating their simple supper the old man told a sorry tale. Once he and his wife had been prosperous, with manservants and maidservants, but things had gone from bad to worse and that year their oat crop had failed – the oats on which they depended for porridge. Their old red cow had died and their only son Hood had been forced to leave to seek his fortune in King Rolf's city.

'Your son is at King Rolf's court then?' asked Biarki.

'That's right sir.'

'I'm bound there myself, so tomorrow you can point out the way.'

Next morning Battle-Biarki was given proper directions and rode off but not before he had left a little leather bag with a few gold pieces for his host and hostess as well as a promise to take their greetings to their son.

It was evening again by the time Biarki reached King Rolf's city and palace-hall. Without a word to anyone he stabled his horse in one of the king's stalls and walked into the palace. It was getting near supper time and the servants were laying platters on the trestle tables. It was rather dark inside. In a sheltered corner he saw something very strange indeed. A scullion was passing.

'Stop!' he cried, 'Are my eyes deceiving me or is that a mountain of bones?'

The servant said, 'Your eyesight is good, your worship. You do see a bone heap.'
'Then where are the scavengers?' asked Biarki angrily. 'Why! That heap is a metre or more high!'

As Biarki walked up to the heap his nostrils detected a stale offensive smell of putrid meat and he saw a hand come from the centre of the pile and place a bone on top. It teetered for a moment then rolled forward and stopped by Biarki's foot. A tuft of dishevelled hair followed by a pair of frightened eyes appeared above the rim of the heap and he saw the dirty face of a youth.
'What by Thor and thunder is this?' shouted Biarki. 'Who are you, and why are you cowering in a filthy heap of stinking bones?'

The youth said, 'My name is Hood sir. But they call me Trembling Hood.'
'So this is how you are making your family's fortune is it?' asked Biarki. 'By amassing a treasure of dirty stinking bones?'
'They're not all stinking, your worship. Some are fresh. I get a new lot with each meal.'
'You get a new lot with each meal? What do you mean?'
'Well sir, it's like this sir. King Rolf's men are a bit sportive. Oh I'm not saying anything against them. They have to have their fun, sir! But it's no good for such as me. You see your worship, every time they have a meal, when they've finished picking their bones they throw them at *me*. It's a sort of competition to see who can hit me most times. The only way I can protect myself is by building this wall of bones.'

Biarki stared hard. 'I never heard anything quite as cowardly as this,' he said.
'Trembling Hood, indeed! A fine fortune you'll make while your old mother and father starve.'
'But what can I do sir?' asked Hood. 'Look at this big lump on my left temple – and look at my right eye; it's all puffed and black! That's where Erik Fat Face hit me yesterday after dinner. Don't stop me sir.'

Biarki looked at the lad's pleading face but the thought of Hood being such a craven coward made him angry. He grabbed Hood by the scruff of his neck and pulled him, kicking and screeching, out through the hall door to a nearby pond. He soused him several times in the cold water until the dirt and stink of the bones had disappeared. Then he marched him still dripping wet to a place at the tables. By now the Vikings were busy eating supper and Hood was really living up to his name and trembling till the platters rattled. His eyes were darting this way and that, and every second he was expecting the bones to begin flying through the air in his direction.

Hood whispered to Biarki, 'Look sir! Look your honour! That's Erik Fat Face crouched at the top of the table – that ape of a fellow gnawing a huge knuckle-bone.'

Biarki glanced where Hood had indicated. 'You mean that burly ruffian with the tangled, uncombed hair and the dangling black moustaches, and a nose like a second-hand beetroot?' he asked.

Hood was thoroughly alarmed for Biarki did not lower his voice.
'Oh sir!' he whispered, 'Don't speak so loud!'
'Stop snivelling lad. Erik will think twice before casting bones in my direction. Here, take this juicy chop and eat it up.'

But Erik Fat Face was only biding his time until he had collected enough ammunition. He belched loudly and turned to a benchmate. 'Hey Swain!' he growled, 'Who's that stranger coming into our king's own hall and pushing up to table without a by-your-leave and more than that, insulting us by giving Hood a seat?'
'Don't know Erik. This is the first time I ever clapped eyes on him. Seems a well set-up fellow. He's certainly big – you could say huge. And not without daring.'
'I'll dare him,' said Erik Fat Face, 'you just watch me,' and he held up the knobbly steer's knuckle-bone from which he had just finished tearing the last strip of meat.

Hood ate up his chop with relish. It was the first bite of fresh meat he had had for a long time. He glanced warily in the direction

of Erik Fat Face and immediately dived under the table.

'Look out! Look out sir!' he yelled from the floor, 'Erik's throwing a big bone!'
There was a whistle of air and a loud smack and Hood screwed up his eyes. He began to moan, 'Oh, where's my bone heap? Let me get back to my bone heap!' He stopped when he heard a second whistle of air and a loud thwack followed by a crash of breaking furniture. He peeped from under the table.

Battle-Biarki was standing up, his eyes flashing. There was a gap where Erik Fat Face had been sitting. Biarki had caught the knuckle-bone and flung it straight back at Erik. Hitting him full on the forehead, it had knocked him backwards off the bench and he was lying unconscious in a pile of broken stools. Biarki was shouting, 'Who's next to try his skill against Battle-Biarki? Let him pick up a bone and hurl it this way! You, you who stand beside the tumbled Erik – you appear to be his friend – lift up your bone and throw!'
'Bone sir? Oh you mean this?' spluttered Swain and he gave a sickly grin, 'I was just going to eat this sir. Yes, yes, I'm eating this,' and he started gnawing feverishly.
'Come up Hood,' said Biarki, 'and finish your

meal.' He dragged Trembling Hood from under the table and pushed two Vikings out of the way to make a place for him.

When Erik recovered he was quick to complain to King Rolf Kraki but the king was no fool and sent for Biarki to hear his side of the story.
'Hail stranger,' said the king, 'My henchman Erik tells me that he has split his head, but not by striking it against a door post.'
'With respect, your majesty, the matter is one of indifference to me.'
'What is your name, stranger?' asked King Rolf Kraki.
'Men call me Battle-Biarki, sire.'
'Then, Battle-Biarki, will you stay here and be my man?'
'King Rolf, I will not object to that. That is why I came to your court. After what has happened I am not so sure.'
'Speak plainly, man,' said the king.
'I came to serve you freely, but now I have a condition. That the youth known as Trembling Hood shall be your henchman too.'

The king and his attendants could not refrain from laughing, but at last King Rolf said, 'Silence! I can see no glory in Hood, but I am at least willing to give you until Yule for him to prove himself.'
'Thank you, your majesty,' replied Biarki.

The dark days and nights of winter were a rather uneasy time at King Rolf Kraki's stronghold. For three years running a winged monster had been in the habit of flying from his den to devour the king's cattle. Presumably the dragon (for such he appeared to be) woke in the middle of winter from his hibernation and felt hungry. He left his lair and, provided no-one attacked him, only cattle were lost. The previous year, seven berserks drunk with mead and in their fighting frenzy had rushed out into the snow, and the dragon had killed them all.

The night before Yule King Rolf's retainers were sticking close to the longfires. The doors were bolted and barred. An old man said doubtfully, 'When I was a lad Yule was a time of joy and jollity. Not now. Not now.' He looked fearfully over his shoulder.

'Has IT been heard of yet this winter?
I've been watching and waiting for IT – but
I've heard nothing.'
'Hush old man! Speak of IT and maybe you'll
draw IT here.'
Battle-Biarki asked, 'What is this IT you are
so fearful about?' They told him.
'Don't speak of it again,' said one, 'It's my
belief the creature's dead or we should have
heard of it before now.'
'It only comes at Yule,' said the old man.
'It will never be seen again . . .' the words
were hardly out of the man's mouth when
violent scratching and snuffling were heard at
the hall door. Immediately there was
a hubbub in the hall and stools were knocked
over as the men panicked.
'IT'S here!' they shouted, 'the beast's here at
the hall door! Come on! Down into the
cellars everyone! Open the trap! Escape!'
King Rolf Kraki strode in.
'Silence! Silence!' cried the king. 'What by
Thor and thunder does this uproar mean?'
'Your majesty, the beast is here! The winged
monster is trying to get in! IT's at the door!'
The sniffing continued and the scratching
grew louder.
'Quiet men!' cried King Rolf Kraki. 'Let me
hear it!' The snuffling turned to a whining.
'Craven cowards!' said the king. 'Call
yourselves men! This is no monster! Pluck
up your courage!' The noise outside changed
to a yelping. 'You all know that today I
went hunting; and what you hear now is my
Irish wolf-hound Gunnar! Open the door
and let him in!' The retainers did as the king
ordered and a great red wolf-hound bounded
in with snowflakes on his long coat. He
shook himself and fawned round the king's
calves. 'Good boy! Good boy!' said King Rolf
and continued, 'Listen men! thrice in
three years the monster – bar that door
securely – the monster has attacked us.
I expect you to fight your equals; I demand
that you shall fight my enemies. You must
fear no man . . . But a monster? Who without
spells and enchantments can prevail
against a monster? Therefore it is my order
that from now until Yule is past our palace

doors shall be barred and double-barred from
dusk to dawn. No man shall wander out
– except at his own peril.'
Trembling Hood said quietly to Battle-
Biarki, 'There master; I told you about the
monster and you wouldn't take my word.'
Biarki said, 'Monster indeed! You and I will
teach this monster a lesson.'
'Oh no sir! Not me sir!' said Hood in alarm.
'Yes, you Hood, it'll make a man of you.
What kind of a beast is he?'
'Well, those who've seen him and got away
say he flies through the air on scaly wings
and the wind whistles as he beats his brazen
pinions! From his sooty nostrils stream flame
and stinking smoke! Sir, he roars! When
he alights he swinges his tail and his eyes stick
out like blazing carbuncles!'
'Have you yourself seen him, Hood?'
'No sir, but Erik Fat Face said . . .'
'Never mind such traveller's tales. When you
yourself have seen the monster . . .'
'I don't want to see him, sir!'
'But you shall my lad, you shall,' said Biarki
and that night when everyone had lain down
to sleep and the fires had sunk low Biarki
crept up to the double-barred doors dragging
Trembling Hood behind him. Very quietly
he withdrew the bars from their massive iron
sockets, opened the doors enough to let the
pair through, closed them behind him and
dragged the unwilling Hood to the king's

cattle fold. Hood hid behind a tree stump.

At last Hood said, 'I'm cold sir. I'm shivering. We've been here hours and I'm sure the monster won't come tonight. Shall we go back?'

'Come closer lad. Here, snuggle into my cloak. We'll wait till dawn.'

'Look sir, Biarki your worship, the dawn *is* breaking. See there's a glow in the sky. Over there behind the trees. Shall we return now?'

'It seems early yet for dawn. Maybe it's the moon rising.'

'No sir, the moon rose hours ago. It's new and it rose and set like a silver nail paring. No your worship. That's dawn.'

'Since when did the sun rise in the west?'

Hood let out a screech. He scrambled to his feet and was almost over the fence before Biarki caught him by the seat of his pants.

'No Hood. You will never run away again,' said Biarki and he forced the youth to stand his ground. Very soon they heard the beat of wings and smelt sulphurous smoke and as the shadow of the creature passed backwards and forwards over them the terrified cattle stampeded round and round. Lowing and bleating mingled with the thunder of hooves, the rattle of scaly wings and the hissing breath of the dragon. Biarki yelled above the noise, 'The dragon! See lad, it hovers in mid air! It begins to drop! Now comes the trial! Either we kill this beast or we die in the

attempt! The wind is thick with smoke and cinders! Come – this way, this way!'

'No, no, no,' whimpered Hood but Battle-Biarki drew him to where the fires shone through the fog of smoke. The dragon landed in the snow with a muffled thud.

'Stand by me while I attack!' yelled Biarki and his long sword clanged on the brazen hide. His iron shield protected him somewhat from the flames but soon it began to glow and he could feel the heat on his fist.

'Hood! Hood! You'll have to help me! It's no use, my sword won't bite into those brassy scales!' But by this time Hood had his foot on the bottom rail of the stockyard fence and was ready to climb over.

Hood cried, 'I told you so! I told you you'd be killed!' The youth turned round to see the warrior who had befriended him about to be destroyed. 'By Thor!' whispered the lad, 'I can't watch him be burned alive. Look out sir! He's lashing out at you with his tail. Jump! You foul beast!' he shouted, suddenly angry. 'I'll smash you . . .' and he ran back from the fence, stumbling through the deep snow and shouting to Biarki, 'It's no good slashing with your sword on his iron neck! Go in under his wing. Under his wing! There are no scales there!'

'Keep back boy!' yelled Biarki, 'The flames will scorch you!'

'I'm all right!' cried Hood, 'Under his wing I

tell you! Here, lend me your dagger sir!
That's it. Give it to me. Now, as he raises his
wing I'll plunge in the knife!'
'Right up to the hilt lad! By Thor, I believe
you've killed him!'

Trembling Hood had indeed slain the
dragon. Its legs folded under it, its ribbed
wings flopped limp like those of a sleeping
bat, its wrinkled neck lay prone in the snow
and a last puff of smoke snorted from its
nostrils.
'You saved my life Hood, and you killed the
dragon *and* you found your manhood – your
name shall no longer be Hood; but Manhood!
It's only fitting.'
'It was all your doing, sir,' said Hood. 'I was
running away until I saw you in difficulties.
Then I couldn't. Thank you, thank you. I'll
do anything to repay you.'

Battle-Biarki was delighted with the night's
work and the effect it had had on Hood. But
he was not yet finished. He made Hood cut
out the dragon's heart and eat a little of it to
give him further courage. Then he unfolded
a surprising plan.
'It's no use *telling* King Rolf that you are a
man now,' said Biarki. 'We have to *show* him
and his Vikings that it is so. Otherwise they
would never believe it. Here's what we will do.'
He told Hood to tear palings and
wooden bars from the fence and push them
under the dragon's wings and neck to prop
them up. When they had finished, the dragon
seemed to have come alive again. 'Now, back
to the palace!' said Biarki and they crept in
as silently as they had left and double-barred
the door once more.

They waited for ten minutes, then they both
shouted at the top of their voices,
'Wake up! The dragon's here!' The Vikings
were very soon falling over each other and
the furniture, and King Rolf appeared, roused
by the noise and rubbing the sleep out of
his eyes. Biarki was struggling to open the
door against a dozen men who wanted to keep
it shut. The king said: 'What news?' and Biarki
shouted above the hubbub, 'Sire, the beast is
here devouring your majesty's flocks and
herds! The dragon is here!'

'Yes, yes!' yelled a number of Vikings.
'Look! See how it tears them limb from limb!
The beast has broken down the stockyard
and gorges itself on the cattle!'
'Has any man gone to the attack yet?' asked
King Rolf.

There was silence. Then Erik Fat Face said
awkwardly, 'No sire, we obeyed your
orders, sire.'
'Then I'll go myself,' said King Rolf.
'King Rolf Kraki!' said Biarki, 'Everyone
knows your bravery. You have no need to
prove it. But here is someone who will go in
your place – Erik Fat Face!'
'I, your Majesty?' stuttered Erik, 'Oh yes –
well no. You see, last night when leaving
your revels I slipped against a stool and
sprained my ankle. See, sire, how swollen it is.
I dare scarce set my foot to the ground.
I'll show you . . .' and he hopped back into
the palace and disappeared.
'See your majesty,' said Hood, 'he takes care
to limp away from the direction of the
dragon.' The men laughed uneasily. 'But if you
will lend me your famous sword Conqueror
I myself will slay the monster!'

Neither Rolf nor his henchmen could
believe their ears and it took all Biarki's
powers of persuasion to get the king to lend
Hood his sword. Of course the outcome
was obvious to two of those present and very
soon Hood returned dragging the beast's
head behind him.
'Now then,' said King Rolf Kraki, 'long ago
I promised a bag of gold and half my cattle
to the man who slew the dragon. That
promise I shall keep. But where is Hood?'
'Let his new name be Manhood your majesty,'
said Biarki.
'Where then is Manhood?'

A Viking cried, 'Sire, look yonder where he
runs! He is performing another miracle
with your famous sword! First he slew the
dragon with it and now he's curing Erik Fat
Face's sprained foot! Look how Erik runs
away from Manhood with no sign of a limp!'

So both Battle-Biarki and Manhood became
King Rolf's men and served him well until
they were called to Valhalla.

Fenrir the wolf is bound

After the World Serpent had been cast into the ocean and Hel had been banished to Niflheim, the problem of what to do with Loki's third offspring the wolf cub Fenrir remained. Like all young things, the cub was at first lovable and cuddly and all the goddesses cried 'Ooh!' and 'Ah!' when they saw him and wanted to pick him up. So Odin allowed Fenrir to be kept at home in Asgard.

It was not long before Fenrir began to growl and snap and show his teeth, which were growing faster than anybody could remember teeth growing before. Heimdall said, 'That animal is going to give us trouble' but Freya cried, 'No he isn't! He's only playful.' She did not think he was so playful after he had almost worried her feather coat to pieces. It took her a month to repair it. 'Well, perhaps we ought to consider putting him on a chain,' she said.

When his feeding time came the wolf was so ravenous and fierce that only Tyr dare offer him food. Every day he put on more and more weight and still seemed empty. Nothing but a whole calf would satisfy his greed. After he had gobbled the flesh he would gnaw the bones with frightful crackings and crunchings until his presence in Asgard became more than the gods could endure.

But that was not all. Prophecies had foretold that Fenrir was destined to do the Æsir irreparable harm, so they concluded they had better find some way of keeping him under control. Odin gave the order that a chain should be made in their own workshops. It was a very famous linked fetter which is known to this day as Loding. They gave Tyr the job of persuading the wolf to try it on as a sort of game.

Tyr said, 'We want to see how strong you are,' and after he had been fed, Fenrir agreed to have the bond fastened on him. His hind legs were accordingly shackled. The wolf looked over his shoulder and yawned. He gave one kick and the fetter flew out of the window, just missing Tyr's head.

There were a few misgivings after that. But the gods manufactured a second fetter which had double the strength of the first and they called it Dromi which means *The* Fetter, for they reckoned this one would certainly work. They asked Tyr to coax the wolf into trying it on.

Tyr gave him a very tasty meal of half a dozen fat sheep and when Fenrir was fed to satisfaction the god said offhandedly, 'Oh, the Æsir have been amusing themselves again, and they have had a bet with me that you couldn't break out of this fetter I have here. You wouldn't let me lose my wager would you?'

By now Tyr was the wolf's only speaking acquaintance in heaven, so the young monster carelessly looked at Dromi out of a sort of contemptuous kindness to his feeder. Tyr said, 'Your strength is being talked about not only in Asgard but in Midgard too, and even in Jotunheim. I don't think you should have any trouble with this.'

The wolf saw that Dromi was much more powerful than Loding but he also believed that since he had smashed Loding his own strength had increased fourfold. There was only a small risk and he decided to run it for the sake of enhancing his fearful reputation. He allowed Tyr to shackle him. Then he pretended to fall asleep.

The Æsir crowded round rubbing their hands with glee. At last they had succeeded in binding the wolf. Fenrir opened one eye and slowly stretched his hind legs. The fetter fractured with a loud *crack* and the wolf rolled over onto his back like a playful puppy before suddenly springing to his feet with a hideous snarl. The gods started back, and the wolf rolled over again unable to contain his terrible laughter.

Odin had to find some way of binding the wolf and he decided to send Frey's boyhood friend and servant Skirnir to a certain dwarf who lived in the land of the dark elves. This dwarf was known as a necromancer and master craftsman, able to employ magic in his trade.

98

Skirnir told the dwarf in his smithy under the ground just what was wanted. This dwarf had eyes as big as saucers and his head was so full of brains it was nearly three times as large as his crooked body.

'Only the most bizarre and outlandish ingredients will combine to make such a fetter as you desire,' the dwarf told Skirnir, 'and the making will take some time. Come back in a month.'

As the weeks went by the wolf was becoming more and more obnoxious. The fact that he had broken Loding and Dromi allowed him to make all kinds of demands and it was feared that before long he would be asking to sit in Odin's own seat at High Nest. At the month's end Skirnir hurried back to the land of the dark elves and the dwarf.

The dwarf said, 'The fetter is ready and I will tell you what it is made from. I have compounded it of six ingredients so skilfully combined you cannot see where one begins and the other finishes. Make certain one end is not joined to the other before the time of the binding and make equally certain it doesn't come round you or anybody else but the wolf or you'll be bound for ever.'

'What are these wonderful ingredients?' asked Skirnir.

'I said I would tell you: first there is the noise of a cat's footfall, then the beard of a woman, the roots of a mountain, the nerves of a bear, a fish's breath and the spittle of a bird – yes, that's the sixth, a bird's saliva.'

'I can't believe it,' said Skirnir, 'nobody ever heard the clip-clop of a cat's feet and women certainly don't have beards, nor fishes breath, nor mountains roots. These things simply do not exist.'

'That's why it took me a month to find them,' said the dwarf. 'Once I had the materials the actual mixing wasn't too difficult. Now, here, take the bond – and be careful.' He handed Skirnir what appeared to be a thread as

soft and smooth as silk. Skirnir rode back to Asgard with considerable misgivings.

The gods were equally dubious when they saw the thread but Odin said the dwarf had a cast-iron reputation as a master craftsman so they should at least try the bond out. A group of the more hardy of the Æsir, including Odin and Tyr, asked the wolf to go with them into the Underworld and row over the dark lake called Amsvartnir to the island of Lyngvi. On that island, Tyr told the wolf, was a herd of such fat, juicy cattle, he would be able to have the picnic of his life. Oh, and another thing, they had a little silken fetter they wanted him to try on for size.

Fenrir allowed himself to be persuaded and when they had rowed out to the dark island he asked where the cattle were. Tyr said, 'We all wondered whether you might like to try this bond on first. It'll give you an appetite,' and he asked Odin to show the bond. The Æsir passed the thread round from one to the other and some of them said it must surely be a little stronger than it appeared from its thickness and they tested it with their hands but couldn't break it.
'Hm,' they said, 'the wolf ought to be able to break this.'
'What do you call this ribbon?' asked Balder.
'It's name is Gleipnir,' replied Tyr.

The wolf said, 'I don't exactly see how I'm to make a name for myself breaking this bootlace – by shattering so frail a rope of sand. But if, on the other hand, a deal of craft and cunning have gone into the making of the bond, then let it seem as soft as it likes – it doesn't come near *my* legs.'

The gods protested that he could not fail to tear such a feeble thread apart in a moment, especially when on two former occasions he had broken great fetters of iron. 'And in fact,' they said, 'if you find you can't slit it then you'll no longer be in a position to frighten us gods and we shall, of course, set you free.'

The wolf observed, 'If you do bind me in such a way that I'm unable to break free, I know in my bones you won't be in a hurry to help me out. I'll tell you what: I'm not over eager to let that bond tie me up. But if you

really are determined to try my mettle, well, let one of you lay his hand between my fangs as a guarantee that you don't intend to double-cross me.'

At this the gods glanced anxiously at one another and at the wolf's snarling, open mouth. Certainly, none of them intended to risk losing his hand. At last Tyr volunteered. He thrust out his right fist and laid it between the wolf's jaws.

The thread called Gleipnir was joined round the wolf's haunches and for good measure twisted about his front paws. When he kicked out, the bond tightened round him, and the more he struggled, the tighter it grew until (as far as he could with Tyr's hand in his mouth) he screeched in agony. Tyr felt the iron teeth biting into his wrist and made ready for the worst. It was clear that the fetter's magic was greater than Fenrir's strength and the wolf was bound for ever. All the Æsir laughed aloud with relief; all that is except Tyr. He lost his hand.

When the gods saw that the wolf was indeed safely bound they took the chain they had attached to the fetter and fastened him at the foot of a lofty crag which had its foundations miles below ground. Then they took an enormous boulder and pile-drove the crag still deeper into the earth, using the boulder ever afterwards to weigh down the crag. The wolf gaped terrifically, struggled madly and tried to bite; so they wedged a sword between his jaws, the pommel at his bottom jaw and the point transfixing his palate. And there he lies until the Ragnarok.

Gylfi said, 'I wonder the Æsir didn't finish the wolf off altogether instead of living in hourly expectation of something evil from him.'

High replied, 'The gods so valued their mansions and shrines that they were loathe to pollute them with the blood of the wolf, even though the prophecies said he would bring Odin's end.'
'Well,' said Gylfi, 'it seems the gods were no better than men at knowing what is good for them.'

His informants did not answer.

How Thor got his hammer

Many exciting and amusing stories are told about the rollicking, red-haired god Thor, the giant-killer. Frequently Loki took part in his escapades but occasionally the Mischief Maker found himself out of favour.

One night in Asgard Loki had difficulty in going to sleep. When he did go off it was not long before he woke again and for some hours he tossed and turned on his lumpy mattress. Just before dawn he could stand it no longer; he crawled out of bed with ruffled hair and bags under his eyes and pulled on his clothes feeling thoroughly spiteful.

He walked out into the deliciously scented air at the moment when the fresh dew was forming and he hated everything. He came to the palace of Thor and as the doors were locked (Thor being away in the east hunting trolls) he scrambled up a trellis supporting a lovely blossoming wisteria until he reached an open window. The window was one of the many in Sif's bedroom. Bent on mischief, Loki cocked a leg over the sill and climbed through. His ferrety eyes swept the daintily furnished room. The golden haired goddess was fast asleep and her rippling hair lay like shining silk along the pillow and overflowed onto the white damask sheets. The spite in Loki's heart was joined with a malicious envy and quite forgetting the vengeance he might expect from Thor, he softly crept to Sif's dressing-table, picked up a pair of jewelled scissors and proceeded very carefully and quietly to cut off all the precious golden hair.

When he had finished, the goddess's head was left with nothing but a downy stubble; she looked for all the world like a shorn dandelion clock. She stirred and began to wake up. Loki quickly bundled the long thick ropes of hair into his tunic and hurried to the window. As he climbed out, one of his sandals fell off and he had no time to retrieve it. He hastened away under cover of the shadows just before dawn broke and safely gained the shelter of his own palace.

When Sif woke her shrieks and wails roused all her neighbours. Freya came and Nanna, Balder's wife and both of them did their best to console her. Nanna picked up the sandal by the window.

'Look,' she said, 'the culprit left his shoe.
If we can find its match we'll have our man.'
'How will that help me?' sobbed Sif, 'I'll
still be as bald as a coot! Where's Thor?' she
cried. 'It's his fault! He should be here with
me not enjoying himself hunting trolls and
bagging ogres!'

By chance Thor did return home that very
morning and when he saw his beautiful wife's
disfigurement he was furious. He was shown
the sandal.

'Loki, by Jormungander!' he shouted and the
windows rattled with his roar. 'I'd know that
fancy footgear anywhere! I'll kill him! I'll
break every tooth in his head and every tiny
bone in his body!' And he made off in his
boiling fury to carry out his threat. He caught
Loki with one hand by the nape of the neck
and began to shake him.

'Stop! Stop! Please,' gasped Loki through
chattering teeth, 'I'll never do it again! Oh
please stop! I'll go to the dark elves and they'll
make golden hair for Sif better than ever
grew on that lovely head. Yes, she *is* lovely
Thor, very lovely. And she'll be lovelier
still. Oh thank you – thank you – please don't
shake me any more!' But Thor was merely
changing hands. 'Oh, oh, oh,' moaned Loki as
his teeth began again to bang together,
'See, I'll get the d-d-d-dark elves to make a
p-p-p-present for Odin and and one for
F-F-F-Frey as well – perhaps I can get something for you also, Thor!'

Of course the end of it was that by pleading
and promises of presents Loki persuaded
Thor to spare him and as soon as he could, he
left Asgard and made his way to
Svartalfaheim, the world of the dark elves.

Loki was owed a favour by a tribe of
dwarfs called the sons of Ivaldi who lived with
the dark elves. Like all the dwarfs, they were
skilful artists and craftsmen, working the gold
and silver they dug from the deep mines and
ornamenting their treasures with diamonds
and rubies. The sons of Ivaldi did not take
long to create the finest head of golden hair
Loki had ever seen; and in addition they made
a spear for Odin which once released from the
hand would never miss the mark at which it

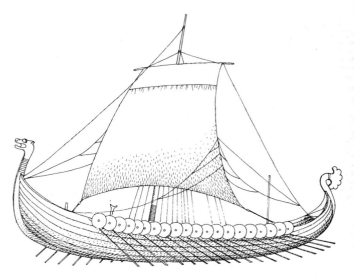

was aimed; and for Frey they wrought a ship
which, when the sail was raised would always
get a favourable wind but when not
required could be folded up and put away in
the pocket like a handkerchief. They called the
spear Gungnir and the ship Skidblade.

With these treasures, Loki quickly regained
his old cockiness and as he was whistling his
way along the tunnels and underground
borings back to the light he happened to pass
the smithy of two famous dwarf brothers called
Brokk and Sindri.

Brokk looked up at Loki from his wrinkled
face and asked him what he was carrying
away from Svartalfaheim. Loki told him and
wishing to brag he said, 'You and your
brother are supposed to be unbeatable as craftsmen but I'm willing to wager my head
you can't make three treasures the equal of
these!'

'Done!' said Brokk without a moment's
hesitation. 'Brother Sindri! Start blowing the
fire, get to work on the bellows!'

'No brother,' said Sindri, 'I'm the elder and
you're the stronger. You blow the bellows
and I'll make the treasures.'

Loki pursed his lips doubtfully. His boast-
fulness was leading him into trouble again.
He stood inside the smithy and watched. Then
he sat down in the shadows away from the
heat and glare of the ruddy charcoal fire.
As far as Brokk and Sindri were concerned he
might not have been there, they were so
engrossed in their work. And after a

few minutes Loki wasn't there – at least not in a form anyone would recognize because it had suddenly occurred to him that he might lose his wager and that meant his head; so he had better do something about it.

When the fire was white hot, Sindri laid a pigskin on the shimmering glow and ordered his brother to keep pumping until he returned and removed the work. He said if Brokk did stop blowing, the craftsmanship would be flawed. Brokk continued to pump the bellows in spite of a sudden agonizing smart caused by a giant horsefly which darted from nowhere, settled on the back of his hand and sucked his blood.

Sindri returned. 'Good,' he said and drew from the fire a real live boar with bristles of gold. The boar grunted. 'Magnificent,' Sindri continued. 'Perfect. We'll call this fellow Gullinbursti.'

For the second treasure, Sindri placed fine gold in the furnace and told Brokk to pump the bellows and not to stop blowing until he came back. He left the smithy and as he did so the horsefly settled on Brokk's neck near his right ear and bit him twice as hard as before. No matter how the dwarf waggled his head the fly would not be dislodged, having bored his sucker well into the tough skin. Nevertheless, the smith continued pumping. 'You appear to be sweating more than usual brother Brokk,' said Sindri, 'is anything wrong? My, oh my! This is a very fine ring!' and he drew from the fire the gold ring which

came to be called Draupnir the Dropper.

A third time Sindri procured material for his work. On this occasion it was iron. He laid the iron in the flames and ordered Brokk to blow again, repeating that if once he stopped everything would be spoilt. Then he left the smithy.

He was hardly away before a huge gadfly alighted between Brokk's eyes and stung his left eyelid so deep and painfully that the blood ran into his eye and he was unable to see. The pain was more than he could bear and he made a grab at the fly when the bellows sank down. He brushed the fly off him just as Sindri returned.

'You'll be lucky if what you have there isn't ruined,' said Sindri, removing a hammer from the glowing coals. He looked at it closely and grunted.

Sindri gathered up the three treasures, the golden boar, the ring and the hammer, gave them to his brother Brokk, and told him to guard them safely and take them to Asgard.

When Loki and Brokk displayed their treasures, the Æsir sat on their judgement seats and agreed that the decision was to rest with Odin, Thor and Frey.

Loki gave the spear Gungnir to Odin, thinking that would be a good move in his favour; he gave the ship Skidblade to Frey; and of course Thor got the golden tresses intended for his wife Sif.

The three gods who were acting as judges were very much impressed by Loki's treasures, and the Mischief Maker began to feel his head was now secure, especially as he was certain something had gone wrong in the making of the dwarf Brokk's third gift – the hammer.

Brokk brought forward his treasures. He gave the massive gold ring to Odin, saying that every ninth night eight other rings, equally precious, would drop from it.

To the god Frey the dwarf gave the boar Gullinbursti. Brokk said it would carry its rider over air and sea, night and day, better than any horse. Nor would it ever be so black, either in the dead of night, or in the underworlds of darkness, that the boar would not have enough light to find the way, his bristles sparkled so.

Then Brokk gave Thor the hammer. He said the god could smite with it as hard as he liked at any target and the hammer would never fail to hit and destroy. Secondly, if thrown, the hammer would return to his hand immediately it had completed its blow. Lastly, it was so small he could, if he wished, carry it inside his shirt. The dwarf coughed apologetically, remembering how he had stopped blowing the bellows. There was one tiny blemish: the handle was a bit short.

The Æsir passed these fabulous treasures from hand to hand and gave appreciative gasps at the fine workmanship and the magic qualities of the gifts. The three appointed as judges put their heads together for a few minutes and after a nail-biting pause (for Loki), Odin announced a verdict. In their judgement, the hammer was best of all the treasures and the finest defence against the frost and mountain giants: the dwarfs Brokk and Sindri had won the wager.

No matter how Loki protested, the gods stuck by their decision. At last the Mischief Maker offered to pay whatever ransom the dwarfs desired in order to redeem his head.

Brokk said, 'No.' He remembered how the horsefly and the gadfly had cruelly tortured him and he was determined to show Loki no mercy.

When Loki realized that he was likely to lose his life he yelled, 'Catch me, then!' and as the dwarf went to lay hands on him he was well out of the way, for he had stolen a pair of shoes which enabled him to run on sea and sky as fast as the speed of light.

Brokk begged Thor to corner the runaway and because he was still bitter over what Loki had done to Sif's natural hair, the god of thunder and lightning agreed. Within seconds Thor had trapped Loki by catching his ankle in a jag of forked lightning.

'Come on! You rogue!' thundered Thor, 'for once you are going to pay your just debts!'

It was a pity that even at the eleventh hour Loki managed to wriggle out of his full punishment, but he did.

When Brokk took up an axe and made ready to chop off Loki's head, the cunning one called on Odin as his blood-brother to witness that it was *only the head* that entered into the wager. Nobody had agreed to include the neck, and therefore Brokk must in no way injure Loki's neck. This might well be a devious argument, but the gods believed they had to uphold it.

The dwarf was frustrated and his wrath was dreadful to see. He determined that even if he could not have Loki's head, at least he would seal his sly lips for ever. He drew from his tunic pocket a thong and a pointed knife intending to sew up Loki's lips. The point of the blade was sharp but it had not enough magic to make a hole in Loki's flesh; the knife just would not go through.

Brokk said, 'It would have been better if I'd had my brother Sindri's bradawl,' and the words were hardly out of his mouth before the awl appeared in his hand. 'Yes, this'll do it!' he said and stabbed a ring of holes all round Loki's top and bottom lips.

The thong Brokk used to sew up Loki's lips was famous ever afterwards. It was called simply Vartari, *The* Thong, and no matter how Loki jerked and tore at it, his mouth remained stitched tightly shut. It was many a long day before he managed to untie Vartari and tear the thong from the holes. Even then his lips were still so sore that he hardly dare speak for months. And that, the gods thought, was a very great mercy.

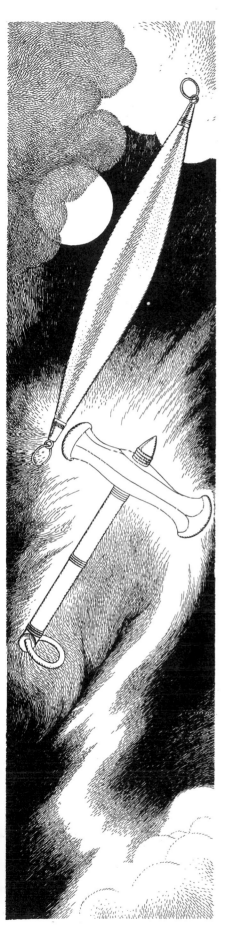

Thor fights the giant Krungnir

Odin's stallion Sleipnir had eight legs and so naturally he was the fleetest steed among gods or men. In addition, he could gallop through the air and over the sea, a considerable advantage to a god in a hurry.

One day when Thor was not at home in Asgard, having travelled east to hunt trolls, Odin had Sleipnir trotted from the stables behind Valhalla, jumped on his back, urged him over heaven's walls and rode across the sky towards Jotunheim. His slowest pace was a hand-gallop, and a fine sight the pair made as Sleipnir's eight legs titupped down the clouds from cumulus to nimbus until he touched ground at Rockyard, the country of a giant called Krungnir.

Being a king as well as a giant, Krungnir regarded himself as a person of some importance. A craggy individual, craggy in appearance, craggy in character, he had a voice like the boom made by an avalanche of frozen snow and boulders. Such avalanches frequently occurred in his ice-capped mountainous kingdom of Rockyard and no doubt he had grown accustomed to raising his voice to compete with them.

Because the sky lit up at Odin's approach, Krungnir was well aware of the arrival of the father of the Æsir but he pretended not to recognize him, crying out insultingly from his battlemented courtyard, 'Halt, who goes there? What manner of man are you, my good fellow, with your swirling cloak, your double-prancing pony and your golden hat? Stand still lad, and tell us your name. Speak up.'

Odin did not reply for he knew that Krungnir could be under no illusions as to who he was. Instead, he cantered round and round the giant king in a way which soon made the giant lose his temper. Krungnir turned on his toe to follow the horse until he was dizzy and had to bellow out, 'Oh yes! I know you! And you have a notable nag there, I'll allow. Don't think I didn't see you riding him over wind and waves!'

Odin cried, 'I'm willing to wager my head there isn't his match in all Jotunheim!'

Now Krungnir himself had a famous stallion called

Golden-Mane and he had him fetched from the stable at once and vaulted straight onto his back intending to pay Odin out for his boasting.

But Odin was ready for him and laid his heels into Sleipnir's flanks. The eight-legged horse soared over Krungnir, Golden-Mane and battlements in one leap, galloped thunderously up to the top of the nearest mountain and out over the broad air in the direction of Asgard.

Krungnir, taken by surprise, suddenly burst into a giant's frenzy. He cruelly cuffed Golden-Mane over the head and the startled stallion's hooves struck fire from the cobblestones as he followed hard at Sleipnir's heels. Necks, backs and tails in one straight line, the two steeds sped through the air, one chasing the other; but Golden-Mane could never quite catch up. When, because of what he saw in front of him, Krungnir did want to stop his horse, he found he had left it too late. Both he and Odin plunged like a pair of shooting stars right over Asgard walls.

Odin slid lightly off Sleipnir's back, slapping him gratefully on the haunch so that he trotted proudly away to his stable. But Krungnir, feeling very uncomfortable, looped Golden-Mane's bridle to the nearest hitching-post: his frenzy had led him to jump right into the stronghold of his deadly enemies the gods. If Thor happened to be at home he knew he would never see Rockyard again. On the other hand, Odin was puffed up with pride and satisfaction at having beaten the giant and at having demonstrated the superiority of Sleipnir, so he patronized Krungnir. 'Come in giant! Come into Valhalla,' he said. 'Make yourself at home. I give you my solemn word as father of the gods that no harm shall befall you in my house.'

This promise at once set Krungnir's fears to rest. He finished tying his horse, walked after the faintly strutting Odin into Valhalla and called loudly for a drink.

It was not long before the heady mead of the gods had filled Krungnir with false courage and he shouted out for larger pots. 'What's the use of these thimbles,' he cried,

'to a giant with a thirst? The gods must have gullets as narrow as earthworms. Hey you, lady,' (this was to Freya the most lovely of the young goddesses) 'serve me my tipple in a lordly jar! Fetch me firkins! Fetch me filderkins! Fetch me whole hogsheads!'

The gods looked at one another in dismay and irritation at this outburst of drunken bad manners. But the laws of hospitality being so strict and Odin's promise so binding, there was little they could do. Loki suggested bringing in the huge puncheons from which Thor was accustomed to drink when at home, and this was done. It was like pouring oil onto a fire already out of hand. With every swallow Krungnir became more objectionable until he was thoroughly fighting drunk. 'D'y'know what I'm going to do, Odin. I'm going to shlay all you gods. Then I'm going to . . . No, No. Wait. I won't shlay Freya an' I won't shlay Thor's wife Sif. They can both come back to Jotunheim with me an' be *my* wives! An' shall I tell you what I'm going to do with this shack called Valhalla? I'm going to pick it up from its miserable foundations an' carry it off on my back to Rockyard. I shall use it for a hencoop!' He drained another of Thor's puncheons and began to sing:

'O when toddling Thor
Waddles in through the door,
I shall laugh till I cry
An' punch him in . . .'

His voice bubbled to a stop as the great doors of Valhalla crashed open and there stood Red-beard Thor, his hammer aloft, come straight from killing trolls.

There was deathly silence except for the tick of a runlet of mead which was dripping from the table to the floor. In his surprise, the giant had slopped over some of his drink. 'Yes your gigantic majesty? Where will you punch him? Toddling Thor, as you call him, is now at the door and ready to waddle – over your dead body!' said the god softly, though his eyes flashed and his arm muscles strained to bursting. But Krungnir defiantly pulled himself together and sang on:

'I shall say I've a pass
From Odin the Ass . . .

' 'sh funny,' he went on, 'Ass means god in your language an' ass in ours means donkey. They're nearly the same thing,' and he laughed loudly and vulgarly.

Thor swung his hammer Mullicrusher towards the spear rafters of Valhalla roof. 'Shtop!' cried Krungnir, 'Odin is lord an' master here, an' he gave me safe conduct! An' let me tell you master Thor . . .' here he disappeared under the table for a minute because he had tried to emphasize his point by crashing his fist on the board, only he missed and turned a somersault among the carved high chairs of the gods. When he had picked himself up he went on, 'You can't hit an unarmed man – well, an unarmed giant. I'll tell you what . . . I'll jusht tell you what . . . I *challenge* you.' This time he managed to wallop his fist on the table so that the drinking-horns danced and jigged about the board. 'I challenge you to single combat. Come to my home at Rockyard an' I'll fight you. An' I'll beat you.' Krungnir staggered to his feet and zigzagged his way to the hall door, pulled himself as best as he could onto Golden-Mane's back and galloped away to Jotunheim.

The news of Krungnir's journey to Asgard and of his coming fight with Thor quickly got round among the giants. The gossip spread like fire in dry grass. It seemed to both the frost and mountain giants that a great deal was at stake for them because Krungnir was their most hardy fighter. If he were to lose the battle, then in future Thor would have it all his own way in Jotunheim. They called a solemn meeting at which it was decided that Krungnir should have some help in the form of a colossal man of clay whom they built as a decoy in Rockyard. He was nine miles and one furlong high and three miles broad under the armpits. They could not get a heart big enough to fit him until they took one from a giant mammoth. Even that was not very steady when the Clay-Man saw Thor. They called him Cloudcalf.

Krungnir was a terrible adversary. His heart was made of stone, shaped like a pyramid with sharp points at all the corners. His head too, was of stone and so was his shield, a rocky circle as high and broad as any cliff face you might see on a desolate sea coast. Krungnir's weapon was a whetstone, a mighty scythe-sharpener and with this over his shoulder he took up his stand at Rockyard alongside the Cloudcalf. He braced his stone shield squarely in front of him.

When Cloudcalf the Clay-Man saw Thor afar off they say he was so desperately frightened that he wet himself.

Thor realized that this particular battle was a little out of the ordinary for him, and instead of charging in fury like a bull he chose to use guile. He stood on the mountains of heaven and called for his servant: 'Run like lightning and tell Krungnir this,' and he whispered a message into the boy's ear.

The boy ran so fast he was only a blur in the sky. When he reached the walls of Rockyard and stopped, he seemed to be a figure materializing out of thin air. He shouted at the top of his voice, 'Ho there, Krungnir! You'll get little benefit standing waiting with your impenetrable shield in front of you like a house-side! Thor has seen you already! He knows your shield is immovable and so he's coming secretly under the earth. He'll topple you down as an earthquake does a tall building.'

Without a moment's thought Krungnir whanged his stone shield under his rock-toed feet and stood on it. Then he brandished his scythe-sharpener with both hands. It was so huge that it stretched from north to south across the sky. At that very moment Thor's anger was fiercest and he let fly with his hammer Miolnir the Mullicrusher. The giant king saw lightning flashes in the west and heard resounding claps of thunder: and at last he saw Thor illumined, blazing in all his divine anger.

Krungnir was holding his whetstone like a mighty quarterstaff but seeing Thor he let go with his left hand, whirled it three times round his head with his right and cast it straight at the god. Like two fiery-tailed comets the hammer and the whetstone met in mid-air and at once the giant's weapon was shattered to bits. Most of the rock fragments

fell smoking onto Midgard and were strewn
about the countryside. But one massive chunk
hit Thor full in the centre of his forehead
and felled him to the ground.

The giant folk, watching from the crags of
Rockyard began to cheer, for they thought
their champion had won the day. They had
failed to reckon with the magic of Thor's
hammer: Mullicrusher, true to its nature did
not falter in its flight but flew to the target
at which Thor had first aimed it – Krungnir's
head. The hammer rebounded *ding-a-dong,*
ding-a-dong upon Krungnir's skull and smashed
it into powder. Where his head had
been there rose up to the sky a cloud of stone
dust. The brutish headless body toppled
slowly forward and one of his legs fell over
the stunned Thor's neck and trapped the god
to the ground.

All this battle smoke, thunder and lightning
was too much for Krungnir's assistant
Cloudcalf: from the head downwards he began
to disintegrate, slithering like a landslide into
a monstrous heap of clay which quivered from
time to time before it settled.

The audience of giants on the rocky shores
of Jotunheim were utterly dismayed and
fled back howling to their mountain fastnesses;
and the Æsir, almost equally put down,
crowded round Thor and tried to lift
Krungnir's leg off his ne   The ponderous
limb lay inert like a m..sy sea mole and not a
god could move it.

At last, Thor's own three-day-old son
Magni the Mighty toddled up. He looked with
great concern at his prostrate father.
At once he seized Krungnir's big toe in
one chubby hand and his little toe in the other
and he cast off the leg. Thor slowly raised
himself to his hands and knees, then stood up
and rubbed his neck.
'It's a pity, father,' said Magni, 'that you didn't
think of sending for me in the first
place. I'd have disposed of this giant for you
without any trouble at all.'
'Good lad,' said Thor, 'I believe you would
have done and I can see you'll be a credit to
your father. And now here's a reward for you:
you shall take the dead giant's horse!'

Thor goes fishing

The god Thor had had a long spell out in the east catching giants and he felt the need of a change. Not that he wanted to stay at home. His wife Sif was delightful, lovely to look at, lively to talk to, but she did not like his untidiness, the way he left his boots and socks lying about and occasionally she got sharp with him. After a time at home, Thor felt he was getting under everybody's feet and he pined for freedom and action. On the occasion of which we are speaking, he had been in Bilskirnir rather longer than usual because the dwarf wheelwrights were still working on one of his chariot hubs so he decided on two things: he would leave his vehicle and goats at home and he would tramp off to the sea to try to find and fight the World Serpent, Jormungander.

Before he left his palace he thought it best to disguise himself somewhat, so he curled his normally unruly hair and beard, dressed in a suit of rather dandyfied clothes and played the part of a young fop. He carefully hid his hammer away in a pouch which he wore at his belt like a sporran.

He left the shores of Midgard and sailed alone right across the ocean until he came to a sandy part of the coast of Jotunheim owned by a giant called Hymir. Thor pulled his boat well above high-water mark, strode up to Hymir's door and because it was evening, boldly asked for a night's lodging. The giant was something of a recluse. He did not like being disturbed and he certainly did not like having to give anything away, although he was a very prosperous fisherman and farmer and had plenty of worldly goods. One of his prize possessions was a herd of silky haired black cattle with white horns.

The fact that Hymir always went fishing in the early morning after he had done the dairy work seemed to Thor an excellent thing. He would propose accompanying the giant when he fished in the hope of seeing the World Serpent.

Grudgingly Hymir accepted Thor as a lodger. The laws of hospitality made it impossible for him to do anything else. Next morning, just before daybreak, Thor heard the giant creaking his way out of bed and fumbling for his clothes in the dark. He was too mean to light a candle. He was going to milk the cows before rowing out to sea for the morning's fishing.

Thor lay back for half an hour and when he judged the dairy chores would be done, he got up and dressed himself. He met Hymir carrying the last two milk churns from the dairy to a running brook where the giant was going to set them in the water to cool.
'You'll be going fishing now, no doubt,' said Thor, 'I'd like to come with you.'
'Don't want any passengers,' grunted Hymir.
'Not as a passenger,' said Thor, 'I mean to row with you and to help you to fish.'
'You don't look much of a one for pulling an oar,' said Hymir, 'not in those trousers.'
'You'd be surprised,' said Thor. 'Tell me, what do I use for bait?'

Hymir nodded his head towards the stockyard where his cattle were munching the early morning feed of hay. 'Help yourself,' he said nastily, meaning there was plenty of dung lying about. Thor chose to misunderstand him. He cut off the head of a steer thinking to himself that even the World Serpent might be tempted with that. Hymir glared but said nothing.

The ill-assorted pair made their way across a belt of pebbles to where Hymir's rowing boat was pulled up onto the sand. Together they launched it, Hymir grumbling all the time muttering, 'I can't see what help I'm going to get from this fellow. If I row out as far as I normally do this puny dandy is going to freeze.'

Thor was losing patience and even thought of getting out his hammer and finishing Hymir off, but he held himself in, being determined to try his strength in quite another quarter.
'Don't fuss so,' he said, 'I don't care how far we row from the shore, I shan't be the first to ask to turn back.'

Thor made himself comfortable on a thwart, picked up a couple of oars and started to row. Hymir rowed forrard in the prow gazing sullenly at Thor's back but no matter how he tried to speed up the strokes he was unable to better his companion's efforts. At last he decided to admit the young dandy was best and said they had come far enough.

'These are the banks where I always angle for flat-fish,' he growled ill-temperedly.

The god knew they would have to press on to have any hope of encountering the Serpent so he cried, 'No, no! Just a bit further! If you're tired, take a rest and I'll row alone.' Hymir bit his lip and they pulled on smartly for another half hour. The giant spoke out a little more vigorously:
'This is far enough! If we go any further from shore we might catch something we don't want – and it won't be a cold!' he cried.

Still Thor refused to stop rowing and once again Hymir had to help. At last, the giant pulled his dripping oars on board and said, 'Stop!'
'Why?' asked Thor.

The giant had to tell the truth. 'Because,' he said, 'we are already above the territory of the World Serpent. Don't you realize it's dangerous to stay around here?'
'If this is good enough for Jormungander then it's good enough for me!' cried Thor. 'This is where we can expect the best catches to be. Get the fishing rods out!' He grabbed the biggest of the giant's rods and a line as thick as his wrist and an iron hook large enough to trouble a whale. 'This'll do for me!' he said and fastened the ox's head firmly onto the hook. He flung the head overboard. It entered the water with a smacking splash and the big round eyes seemed to regard him reproachfully as the head and horns sank slowly down into the depths of the sea.

Hymir himself was forced to fish as well, but he took care to choose a thin little rod with a tiny hook and only a sprat for bait. He had no intention of tangling with the World Serpent if he could avoid it. Like any other anglers, the pair sat hunched in the boat, one watching one side and one the other. In fact Hymir uneasily scanned both sides, he was so frightened that Thor would catch something out of the ordinary.

Down below on the sea bottom the World Serpent was lying with his tail firmly gripped between his jaws. The dim light from the surface clouded over and Jormungander saw two big bull's eyes and a pair of white horns drift slowly down towards him. He raised one of his huge lips, all warty and barnacled, and sucked a hole between his teeth large enough to allow the ox head to be drawn through. It was already halfway down his throat when he felt the hook prong into his gullet. He coughed and a great belch of a billow rose up under the giant's boat and nearly turned it over. But the hook would not come out.

When the Serpent realized he had taken a well baited hook, he threshed about so monstrously that Thor's line and rod were almost jerked out of his hands and the god skinned the underside of both wrists on the rough wood of the gunnel. The smart made Thor fizz with rage and he called up all his divine power and dug in with his heels, bracing both feet so hard against the boat bottom that he hauled the Serpent up to the side!

Nobody ever saw a more blood-freezing sight than Thor did, as his eyes goggled down at the Serpent, and the great beast from below glared up and blew a cloud of poison into the air. They say the giant Hymir blenched, then turned yellow with terror at the sight of the Serpent's tail-filled jaws, the massive teeth, the bulbous eyes, the bladderwrack round his horn, the barnacled neck. And all the time the sea swashed violently into and out of the boat. Hymir had but one thought – to save himself. He grabbed the sharp knife he used for cutting the bait which was swilling about in the bottom around his feet and with a couple of stout hacks chopped Thor's fishing line in two. The sea water swished off both ends of the cord and the World Serpent sank back into the ocean to disappear in a whirlpool of bubbles.

Thor raised his fist in mad mortification. At the very moment of success he had been baulked of his prey. He would have given anything to have had the head and horns of Jormungander mounted and fixed onto one of the walls of his palace Bilskirnir. It was not to be. And perhaps it was just as well, for he had forgotten the dire consequences prophesied if ever the World Serpent's tail should be wrenched from his mouth.

Thor vented his rage on Hymir. He gave him such a sickening blow as he brought down his raised fist that the giant turned a cartwheel out of the boat and the last Thor saw of him was the soles of his feet.

Then the god rowed angrily back to shore and made his way home to Asgard.

Thor in the giants' stronghold

One afternoon Thor harnessed his two goats Toothgnasher and Toothgrinder to his massive chariot and rumbled away from Bilskirnir with Loki the Mischief Maker standing beside him gripping the handrail very tightly. It seemed better to have Loki under direct supervision where he could be kept out of serious trouble. As the sun was setting over the sea they came to earth by a lonely farmhouse and asked the farmer for a night's lodging. During the evening Thor led his goats into an outhouse and slaughtered both of them. After that they were flayed and the joints brought into the stewpot. Thor had invited the farmer, his wife and their two children to share the meal: the son was called Thialfi and the daughter Roskva. They all sat round the table to supper. Thor had spread out the two goatskins on the floor in front of the fire and he told the company to throw the bones on the hides.

Thialfi the farmer's son was overjoyed at the treat, for the times were hard and food was scarce. He had as his share one of the goat's thighbones and he split it open with his knife to get at the tasty marrow.

Thor wanted to be off early next morning and in the darkness before sparrow-peep he got out of bed and pulled his clothes on. He fumbled round for his hammer Mullicrusher and making one or two magic passes with it over the hides and the bones, blessed them: with a rustling and a clicking and the ghost of a bleat, the two billy-goats scrambled to their feet. But, calamity! Toothgnasher was lame of his right hind leg and could only limp. Thor spotted it even in the twilight before dawn and was, naturally, very upset. He shouted that either the farmer or some bumpkin in his family had behaved like a numbskull with the bones: he knew that the thighbone had been split.

The shouting brought the farmer and his family out of their beds and they trembled in front of Thor in their nightshirts like naughty children who have just been caught with their fingers in the honeypot. When the farmer saw Thor's eyebrows sink down over his eyes and then looked into the blazing eyes themselves and from them to the god's knuckles as they suddenly glowed white

– he was clutching his hammer shaft so tightly – well, he nearly swooned. So did his wife and his children Thialfi and Roskva. They all began speaking at once, asking for pardon, and the farmer offered all he possessed in compensation. When Thor saw their terror, he allowed himself to be pacified and accepted the two children as his personal servants.

The god decided he had better leave the two goats in the care of the farmer so that Toothgnasher's leg would have time to mend. Instead of using the chariot he borrowed the farmer's fishing boat and the four of them, Thor, Loki, Thialfi and Roskva set sail over the ocean towards Jotunheim.

It was getting dusk when they made a land-fall and disembarked, pulling the boat well up from the sea. They began to tramp inland, Thialfi (who was a sturdy lad and noted for his speed as a runner) carrying the knapsack which contained their provisions. They soon entered a dark forest with clumps of enormously tall trees and just as it was becoming too black to see, they luckily came across a vast building with a doorway which appeared to stretch right across one end.

The four weary travellers went in and quickly lay down huddled together by one of the walls. In the middle of the night the whole building shook and they were wakened up by what they believed to be a terrifying earthquake. The floor slid this way and that and the walls flapped in and out. Thor struggled to his feet and, staggering about, herded his followers into a smaller side-room leading off to the right about halfway down the hall. The god squatted in the entrance to the side-room, the others further in behind him, all rather shaken. Thor gripped his hammer ready to save himself because outside he could hear a loud murmuring and snorting.

As soon as dawn broke, Thor stepped outside the hall and was astonished to see a monumental figure stretched flat among the trees and fast asleep. The roaring and snorting were caused by the man's snoring – if you could call such a monster a man, for he woke up, sprang to his feet and towered high over the god and looked down at him. It is said that for once Thor was too startled to smite with his hammer and asked lamely, 'Who are you?'

The other replied in a great booming voice which echoed from tree trunk to tree trunk, 'VASTY! And there's no need to ask who *you* are – I'd know that red hair and beard anywhere. Thor of the gods, isn't it? So it was you,' he continued, 'who purloined my mitten. Why did you do that?' He stretched out his hand and picked up his enormous 'mitten'. Thor saw it was what they had taken for a hall during the night. The side chamber was the mitten's thumbstall!

Vasty enquired if Thor and his companions were willing to accept his company on the way and the god had to say 'yes'. So Vasty set about unlacing his own provision bag and started eating his breakfast while Thor and his companions did the same a little distance off. Loki and the two children were rather apprehensive, especially when Vasty said it was only common sense to keep their food together and Thor had to agree. Without a word, Vasty stuffed all their provisions into one bag and threw it up over his shoulder.

For the rest of that day Vasty stalked through the forest without a pause, taking long and measured strides with the others scampering behind rather like mice. At nightfall he looked about for a place to camp and decided on a space beneath a gigantic oak tree. Vasty then said he thought he would not bother with supper but would go straight off to sleep and 'here, catch hold of the provision bag and help yourselves.'

In a twink Vasty was asleep and snoring till the ground vibrated and the leaves of the oak above him fluttered and rustled with each breath he puffed out. Thor at once picked up the provision bag to undo it.

This is, of course, a factual report of the events as they occurred, but what is to be told now must seem suspect: nevertheless, it is perfectly true. No matter how Thor tugged and pulled and snatched and wrenched – he could not untie a single knot and no lace-end of the leather food-bag was any looser than another. When he saw his labour was going all for nothing he flew into a violent rage, gripped his hammer Mullicrusher with both fists, took one step towards the spot where Vasty lay and cracked him over the skull!

Vasty stirred and woke up. He mumbled something about a leaf having dropped on his head and disturbed his sleep. When he saw Thor standing there he asked: 'Had your suppers? Isn't it time you were getting some sleep? We've a long way to go tomorrow,' and he turned over and straight away fell asleep again. Thor joined his companions and he, Loki, Thialfi and Roskva huddled together under another oak tree but were too upset to do more than doze.

About the middle of the night Thor heard Vasty snoring so that the rumble shook the forest. He stood up. Quickly and fiercely he clasped his hammer, tiptoed towards the snorer and aimed a tremendous blow full at the centre of his crown: he even felt the hammer face sink deeply into the giant's head. Vasty woke up at once: 'What's up now?' he grumbled. 'An acorn, I expect. Fell off the tree onto my head.'

Then Thor sat and thought seriously to himself that if he got the chance of a third wallop, Vasty would be the last to know anything about it. He lay down once more with his ear cocked to listen whether Vasty was hard asleep. A little before the grey of dawn he heard Vasty snoring and he shot up and leaped at him, swinging the hammer with all his power and driving it down on the giant's upturned temple. The hammer sank in as far as the helve.

But Vasty only sat up and rubbed his cheek, muttering, 'Curse those dirty birds roosting up the tree! You know, I just realized – half asleep, half awake – the nasty little beggars have messed on me through the twigs! Oh – it's Thor again. So they've wakened you as well, have they?' He gave an enormous yawn and Thor and his companions felt in serious danger of being sucked into a mammoth cave. 'Still,' he went on, 'I suppose it's time to get up and get dressed.' He began to rummage about. 'As a matter of fact, you aren't far now from the stronghold known as Outgard. I've heard you gossiping among yourselves about my not being exactly a midget – well, take this from me: you'll see men a trifle larger still in Outgard. Now, just let me give you some very good advice: don't go showing off. King Loki of Outgard's retainers won't stomach any putting on of airs from such tiny toddlers as you are. Or better still – why don't you turn back? I do really believe that would be your best plan. No?' Thor was shaking his head. 'If you do aim to go on, this is where you turn off to the east. My way lies north to the snow-capped mountains you can see in the distance.' Vasty slung the provision bag across his back and made off into the wood.

Thor and his companions, hungry and irritable, set their best feet forward and soon came out of the forest onto an open plain. Soaring high into the sky they saw a stronghold which could only be Outgard. Even though they pressed back the crowns of their heads onto the napes of their necks they still could not see the battlements. They walked round the walls until noon when they arrived at the main gate and found it blocked by a great grille which they could not move. There were dandelions and nettles growing between the cobblestones, only the dandelions were as big as sunflowers and the nettles as tall as two men. The four slid easily between the bars of the grille.

Their eyes were at once caught by a vast building in the middle of the town square. The door was open so they walked in. They saw crowds of men sitting up to two trestle tables.

Almost at once the four found themselves facing King Loki of Outgard. He sneered: 'Of course, news travels slowly to us here at the back of beyond and I may be making a big mistake: but, is it – can this young bully-boy be Two-Goat Thor? Oh no, no. Surely you should be bigger than this? Come on, now. Is it a joke? You're hiding something, aren't you? There must be far more about you than appears at the moment. Tell you what – here's your chance: say just what talents you reckon you and your mates possess. No-one is allowed to stay very long

here with us unless he's particularly clever in some art or science.'

The one of the party who was bringing up the rear, Loki, feeling famished from not having had anything to eat for a day and a night blurted out, 'I know an art which I'm willing to put to the test. It's that nobody in this hall can eat a good square meal quicker than I can!'

Loki of Outgard looked down his long nose and observed, 'Yes. That *is* something of a feat if you can bring it off. We'll test you.' He bellowed out across the tables that the one called Blazeaway should step onto the floor and pit himself against Loki. Without delay, a long wooden trough was dragged into the hall and piled high with meat, bones and gravy. Loki took up his station at one end and Blazeaway at the other. At a signal from King Loki of Outgard both began to gobble as fast as they could, with the result that they came nose to nose in the very middle of the trough.

Loki had eaten every shred of meat off the bones and lapped up all the gravy; but as for Blazeaway, he had eaten the meat *and* the bones *and* the gravy *and* his half of the trough as well!

The giant king then asked if the young fellow standing there with his cap in his hand knew anything worth knowing and Thialfi, who had never been beaten on Midgard at foot racing, said he was ready to run against anybody.

King Loki said: 'Racing is a noble sport but this young fellow will need to be very fleet footed indeed if he is to win against my local boy.' He stood up and invited the visitors to follow him outside to an excellent race-track and, once there, he whistled for his page-boy called Wit and told him to run a match, best of three, against Thialfi.

The two lads ran a first heat in which Wit gained just enough on Thialfi to be able to turn round and meet him at the tape. Loki of Outgard said, 'Thialfi, you're a good boy; but don't you think you'll have to put just a bit more effort into it if you want to beat Wit?'

The two runners, having got their breath

back, ran a second heat. Wit had sped there and back by the time poor Thialfi was only half way down the track. King Loki said, 'I'm quite certain in my own mind that Thialfi is a good runner, but I just can't see him winning now. Let's find out. They have one more race to go.'

They raced again. At the word 'Go!' Wit was there and back again, while Thialfi had merely lifted one foot off the ground and his mouth had opened not to draw breath but in amazement. Everybody had to agree that the contest had been well and truly decided.

King Loki tutted but said nothing pointed about it though his face spoke volumes. He looked at Thor who was quietly fuming with rage.
'Well,' said the king, 'what particular party piece would you yourself like to give us? There's got to be something – we've heard so much talk about all your exploits.'

Thor said, 'I will drink any champion under the table – anyone at all you care to put forward!'

The king shouted for his cupbearer to bring in the horn they were accustomed to use for drinking contests. Immediately, a young giant pulled in a huge horn which could well have been shed by the Cosmic Cow Authumla. It stretched out all along the floor of the hall and its point disappeared into the shadows. Thor grasped the rim with both hands and found the horn nearly full.

He said, 'It doesn't appear to be over wide at the mouth but I have to admit I've never seen a drinking vessel quite as long as this.'

Loki of Outgard said, 'It's a good horn. We reckon a seasoned drinker can empty it in one draught. Some men take two. Nobody, in our experience, is so unparched as not to be able to down its contents in three tries.'

Thor knew his own drinking capabilities and at that moment he had a fine thirst on him. He began to gulp the liquid down with such huge swallows he believed he would not need to bow his head over the horn more than once. At last, his breath gave out. To see what progress he had made with the drinking, he peeped inside the horn: there seemed to be hardly any difference between the level now and before he had started. Loki of Outgard said, 'Oh, well drunk! Though – I wonder?' He looked at the level of the liquid. He absent-mindedly stroked his huge ear. 'No. I see you haven't drunk to excess. Do you know, if anyone had told me that Thor of the gods couldn't quaff deeper than this, I shouldn't have believed him. I know what you're up to, sly boots, you intend to make quite certain of polishing it off in two goes!'

Thor didn't say a word. He jammed the horn rim into his teeth intending to take the drink to end all drinks – and did so, up to the final squeak of wind in him.

When he took the vessel from his lips and looked, it seemed to him there was even less difference in the levels than there had been after the first draught.

King Loki said, 'What's up now Thor? Aren't you holding yourself back just a bit too much for your last drink? You must drain the horn or we can hardly call you a drinker of note and we certainly can't allow you the sort of inflated reputation you have at home with the gods. Well, not unless you are really good at something else.'

Thor was furious. He rammed the horn halfway down his throat and sucked like a whirlpool just as long as he was able, and when he looked inside the level had certainly sunk considerably, but the horn was by no means empty.

'Pah! It's salty!' cried Thor and he thrust the horn away.

His host said, 'It's obvious that your capacity isn't what we've been led to believe. Is there anything else you would like to try?'

Thor growled, 'I'm game for anything – anything at all! As a matter of fact, the drinks I have just drunk would have surprised the Æsir back home – I'm quite sure of that. There's something funny going on here. What other tricks have you got up your sleeve?'

Loki of Outgard said, 'No tricks, but there is a game we play here, or at least, our young lads do when they want to vie with each other – you know, showing off. Well, they're only boys, so a man should find no difficulty with it – it's picking up my cat.'

Almost at once, Thor and his companions were aware of a cat's body stretching quite across the width of the hall. It was striped, a sort of grey tabby – a giant one, of course. Thor walked straight to it and placing his

right hand under its belly, pushed roughly to the full length of his brawny arm. The trouble was that every time he pushed, the cat arched its back. Even when the god stood on tiptoe and stretched his arm and fingers to their full extent the cat merely lifted one paw off the ground.

Loki of Outgard said, 'I thought as much. The cat is rather a large cat, while Thor is on the short side – stunted even, compared with the giants we are accustomed to.'

Thor snapped, 'Stunted I may be – but let somebody step up quick and wrestle with me! Now I really am angry!'

King Loki glanced along the tables and replied, 'Do you know, I don't see a single giant present who wouldn't consider it beneath his dignity to wrestle with you. I can't think what we should do –' then he added, 'Oh yes, there's my granny! Thor can wrestle with my granny! Give a shout for the old lady Annodomini, and Thor shall try a fall with her. She's often put down men who seemed to me a lot stronger than Thor is.' The very next instant, before Thor had had time to protest, an old, old woman hobbled into the hall. She was white-haired and wrinkled, her eyes were glazed, her back bent double with time, and she appeared so ancient and tottery that a slight draught of wind would blow her away. She was so hard of hearing that King Loki had to put his mouth up to her face and bellow: 'Grandma! I want you to try a hold with Thor of the gods!'

Thor circled round the old lady with mixed feelings but determined to put an end quickly to the farce. He calculated that a combination of demon flying-cannonball and treble nelson back-breaker would be enough. But when they came to grips, the more strenuously the god exerted himself the more rock-like and immovable the old lady stood. Then she herself began to make a move, like a person in slow motion; and finding Thor a bit unsteady on his feet she wrestled all the fiercer. It was not long before she had forced the Thunderer down onto one knee!

King Loki stepped forward to the strugglers. 'That's enough!' he ordered. The

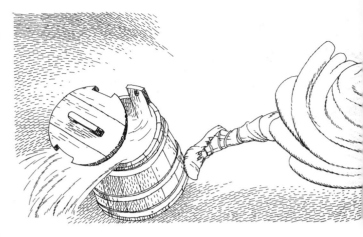

old lady ignored him and Thor's eyes were beginning to pop out of his head. 'TIME! Grandma!' the giant king yelled and pulled her off. She shambled out of the hall. 'Surely,' whispered Thialfi to his sister Roskva, 'she must be one of those wrestlers who perform in disguise – you know, really hard men.'

'Come and eat and drink,' invited King Loki, and the four travellers, rather crestfallen, were shown to seats at the table where they feasted with the best for the rest of the night.

Next morning Thor and his companions got ready to leave. King Loki went with them through the stronghold gates and onto the open plain. As they were about to part, the giant addressed Thor, asking if he was pleased with his trip and if he felt that for once he might have met his match. Thor admitted that he appeared to have been taken down a peg or two. 'And that goes against the grain,' he growled.

Loki of Outgard said, 'Now that we are out of the stronghold I'm prepared to let you into a secret. First, if I can prevent it, you shall never come inside my fortress again, and if I'd known when I first met you in the forest what I know now (that was me in disguise – you remember, Vasty?) I would have done everything in my power to stop you coming into Outgard. For what you accomplished here has brought us all to the very brink of destruction. I'll tell you why – but first, back to the meeting you had with Vasty.

'When, that first night in the forest you tried to undo the provision bag, I had closed it fast with magic wire. When you struck at me three times with your hammer, although the first blow was the least, it would have killed me dead – if only it had landed! Well, you may remember seeing a saddle-back crag by the hall in the forest? And you saw three box-shaped valleys, one much deeper than the other two? Those were the imprints of your hammer. I slipped the saddle-back crag in front of each stroke but hypnotized you so you couldn't see it!

'The same sort of thing happened in the various contests you and your party had with my retainers. Take the first one which your man Loki tried: he was certainly famished and gobbled quickly enough in all conscience! But his opponent Blazeaway – well, *he* was *wildfire* and had no difficulty in burning up the trough as well as everything in it. When Thialfi tried racing the boy called Wit, he was pitting himself against a *thought* out of my head.

'Now you yourself. You drank from the horn and thought you were making poor progress, but strike me dumb! Those draughts were a prodigy – something nobody could have believed possible – because the open end of the horn, unknown to you was plunged in the ocean! And when you come to the sea just look for the tide mark and you'll discover by the empty foreshore just how much you drank away in those mighty draughts!'

While the gods and the two children were regaining their breath and staring in amazement, Loki of Outgard paused and then added, 'You remember when you pushed up the cat? Well, there wasn't a giant there who was not shivering in his shoes! When the animal's foot left the ground they nearly died of terror. That cat wasn't at all what it seemed to you. It was the World Serpent! And we all know what will happen when *its* tail leaves its mouth – the End! Just as marvellous was when you stood firm so long in the wrestling match and only went down on one knee. For there's never been a single person, and never will be to the end of time, who is not finally beaten by the old lady Annodomini: *she* is Old Age.' He paused. 'You'd better think all this over,' he added, 'and please don't come this way again, for I shall always be ready to protect my stronghold with similar spells and other new ones even more powerful.'

By then Thor had recovered himself. He reached into his tunic for his hammer and swung it wildly, only to see in front of him – nothing. King Loki had disappeared into thin air, the stronghold had disappeared, and none of Thor's party had the slightest idea where to start looking for them. So they retraced their footsteps through the forest and sailed back over the sea. Thor collected his chariot and goats (Toothgrinder now fully recovered from his lameness) and they all drove back thoughtfully to Bilskinir.

123

Thor's holiday

Loki had been up to mischief again, and this time he had 'borrowed' the goddess Freya's feather coat without bothering to ask her permission. Bright and early one morning he pocketed the hawk skin, climbed to the battlements of Asgard walls and when he thought no-one was looking, put on the coat and launched himself into the sky. He found it amusing to flutter his wings and stand at one point in the air while all the tiny birds below such as larks and tits fled away in alarm, and the small animals such as field-mice and voles scurried for safety. But he soon tired of this behaviour and struck out across the sky and over the sea towards Jotunheim.

By chance he flew to the great hall of a giant called Geirrod and out of curiosity landed on the roof and made his way inside through an open dormer window. He walked out along one of the roof beams and peeped down to see what was happening. He found it all very amusing. It was like being a fly on the wall, able to watch everyone in secret. A giant servant had lifted the crust of a pie and was stealing the fruit because he thought no-one could see him. Another one was surreptitiously lapping at the cream bowl. They were all supposed to be laying the tables for dinner and soon the giant Geirrod himself came in and sat in his high seat. Before long he was tearing the joints apart and flinging the bones over his shoulder to dogs as big as horses.
'Dirty fellow,' thought Loki, 'no manners. We don't do that in Asgard.'

He leaned forward for a better view and his hawk's chest loosened a deserted swallow's nest clinging to the beam on which he was perched. The nest dropped like a stone into a bowl of curds and whey which Geirrod was just about to attack. The yellow sticky mess was flung up into his face and gummed his eyebrows and beard into an uncomfortable ropey tangle. After his first shock, Geirrod looked up wiping the curds out of his cruel eyes and saw the hawk perched on the cross-beam. His surprise was not diminished nor his anger allayed when he became aware that the bird was laughing at him! An ordinary bird laughing is quite something to see – only parrots and mynahs do it reasonably well. 'Fetch me that bird!' shouted Geirrod to one of his young men and the fellow began to swarm up the wall using every knob and projection to help his ascent. Loki watched the man with increasing amusement, especially when he missed a footing and hung with one hand, in danger himself of dropping into Geirrod's dinner. The Mischief Maker had it all planned out. As soon as the climber reached the end of Loki's beam, the 'hawk' would fly to the next beam and the man would have to go down and start all over again.

There was only one snag, which Loki didn't know about. As the climber reached his beam, Loki spread his wings and stirred up a gale of wind and dust but failed to rise from his perch! The giants were in the habit of pasting bird-lime along the beams to discourage starlings and sparrows and Loki found his claws firmly stuck in it. No matter how he flapped and fluttered he was unable to break free and the young giant roughly grabbed one of his flailing wings and snatched him off the beam.

Very soon they were both on the ground and Loki was in front of the giant Geirrod expecting the worst. The giant looked into the 'hawk's' eyes and at once recognized them for those of a man. He knew then he had to deal with a shape-shifter and he boomed: 'Who are you! Tell me your name quickly or you die!' Loki suspected it would be the worse for him if he revealed who he was so he remained dumb, except occasionally to let out what he hoped was a hawk-like croak.

Geirrod growled, 'Very well, then. Lock him in a cage with no bird-seed or water. When he's hungry enough, he'll twitter.'

After three months, Loki could hold out no longer and he agreed to tell Geirrod who he was. The giant was delighted to have the Mischief Maker in his power and he said, 'Now then, you can make a bit of private mischief for me. I have, in fact, almost decided to kill you out of hand. But provided you swear by Odin's head to bring

about a thing I have dreamed of for years, I will spare your meddling life.'
'What is that?' whined Loki.
'You know, of course,' said Geirrod, 'that the greatest enemy and destroyer of us giants is the god Thor. Now he is only successful because he owns the invincible hammer and the girdle of strength. I want you to bring him here to me *without* either his hammer or his strength-increasing belt.'
'But you would be able to kill him,' said Loki.
'That's the idea,' said Geirrod, 'you catch on quickly. Now let's see how clever you really are. It's him or you,' and he grabbed the hawk in his two big hands and started to wring its neck.
'Stop! Stop!' squawked Loki, 'I'll bring him! I swear by Odin's head I'll bring him!' and after he was satisfied with the oaths, Geirrod let him go free.

When he got back to Asgard Loki spent days nervously wracking his brains for a way to lead Thor into Geirrod's trap. Thor would never go out on business unless he had his hammer, his belt and usually his special iron gauntlets as well. Loki knew that for certain. Suddenly a thought struck him – 'on business' yes, but what about 'on holiday'?

Loki called round at Bilskirnir and said he was seriously thinking of going on a holiday. He had just had a new boat built and he wondered if Thor would like to take a few days off and help him to crew it? He told Thor that the boat had recently come off the stocks at Niord's seaside home and that it had a newly invented steering-oar he wanted to try out. Of course, Thor was like a young boy, only too eager to get away. He dressed in a raw sheep's wool sweater and sailor's slacks, not caring for once about leaving his hammer and strength-increasing belt behind.

Loki and Thor very quickly put to sea with a fresh off-shore wind and before long were halfway across the ocean to Jotunheim. The wind increased to gale force and as the boat had only the one square sail it was impossible to tack and turn about. They were

driven onto the shores of Jotunheim and, as the sun was near setting, they had to look around for a night's lodging.

By chance they had landed at a little jetty owned by a giantess called Greeth.

Greeth was a good-looking woman but more than that, she was rumoured to be an enchantress. However, she quickly made the two travellers welcome and asked what business they had with Geirrod.
'We have no business with Geirrod or any other giant,' said Thor. 'We're on holiday. Why do you ask?'
'But your friend has business with Geirrod,' said Greeth looking hard at Loki. 'The gossip around these parts is that this young man was a prisoner in Geirrod's Garth for more than three months and that he was only let out under certain conditions.'
'What's all this about, Loki?' demanded Thor, suddenly suspicious. In five minutes, Loki had confessed everything, adding,
'What could I do, Thor? Geirrod was going to kill me –'
'Yes,' replied Thor, 'and now I'm going to do the job for him!'
'No! Please no!' whined Loki, and Greeth said, 'Don't you worry your red head Thor, for I'm sure I can help you. Here you are, and no doubt Geirrod's spies know of your coming; so go on boldly to Geirrod's Garth. Now I know that Geirrod is a crafty old giant and he believes he will get the better of you this time. As it happens, I myself own a strength-increasing belt and a pair of gloves similar to yours. You're welcome to borrow them. True, I don't have a hammer, so you'll have to use your wits. But my magic wand ought to stand you in good stead.'

Thor thanked Greeth and accepted the loan of her three treasures. Next morning he and Loki set out into the high mountains on the road to Geirrod's Garth. Before long they came to a noisy and fiercely running river of ice-cold milky melt water known as Vimur. They waded in with the water well above the knees of Thor's sailor's slacks. And this was hardly at midstream. Just as they were negotiating the underwater rocks at what appeared to be the deepest part, the water began to rise suddenly and swiftly until in three seconds it was under their armpits. Loki could only save himself by hanging onto the tail of Thor's hood, and Thor could only keep his feet by snapping on Greeth's belt of strength and propping her wand downstream to support them. As the waves began to splash over his head, Thor glanced upstream to where the river was roaring through a ravine. There he saw Geirrod's daughter the giantess Yelp channelling the water from several mountain torrents into the river, causing the flood.

Thor held Greeth's wand with his left hand and with his right fumbled on the river bed for a large pebble or rock. He found one and hurled it dripping at Yelp.

A few strides later and he had reached the farther bank. He grabbed a rowan tree leaning out over the edge of the rushing water and pulled himself and Loki onto the river bank.

When Thor and Loki did reach Geirrod's Garth and, still damp and uncomfortable, asked for lodging, they were shown into a stinking goat house whose only furniture was a three-legged stool used for milking. Thor sat down on it and began to take off his sodden boots. Then he thought he was going dizzy; the walls were moving! Suddenly he realized it was not the walls but the stool which was shifting. It was rising rapidly off the ground and about to trap him like a fly against the ceiling. Fortunately, he had rested Greeth's wand between his legs when he sat down and he speedily gripped it with both fists and stuck it up at the roof, pushing down with all his belt-increased might. He felt the stool give way under him. There was a tremendous crash followed by screeches. Geirrod's two daughters Yelp and Clutch had been hiding under the stool and the god had squashed them both flat on the goat-dunged floor.

Of course, Geirrod was quite unaware that Thor was ready for any attack and having told a servant to fetch the god into his great hall, the giant prepared to reverse their roles

and make a name for himself as a god-killer.

There was a longfire burning the length of the hall and Geirrod was sitting like a rugged mountain in his high seat at the far end. His hair stuck out like bramble bushes and the few parts of his warty face which were free from whiskers were knobbed like the scree at the bottom of a cliff. His arms were the colour of oak tree boughs and ribbed with veins like ivy.

'Come in!' he bellowed, 'and catch hold of this!' He reached with a pair of tongs into the fire and withdrew from the flames a white-hot bar of iron which he had been preparing like an ingot in a furnace for Thor's reception. As he poised the glowing rod above his head, it melted the spiders' webs in the rafters and charred the nearest beams. 'Yes!' he roared, 'grab this!' and flung it from the end of the tongs in spear fashion full at Thor's midriff.

You can judge the surprise, the dismay and then the fear which chased each other across Geirrod's warty face as he saw the flying burning ingot stop, so it seemed, in mid-air. Thor had caught it two-handed in Greeth's famous gloves. Then the god gave a great shout of laughter, tossed the bar above his head and as it came down horizontally, clutched it in the middle to get a better balance. Geirrod realized with horror that the white-hot spear was coming back at him. He shot up so quickly that his high seat fell over backwards with a crash. In spite of his bulk, he quickly darted behind a thick iron pillar.

Like a comet in reverse, with all its fire in front, the flaming iron bar flew back the length of the hall and pierced the metal pillar, the giant, and the wall behind him. It was all over in a moment and the astonished Geirrod was dead.

Thor picked up a drinking horn from the nearest trestle table and drained it. 'Tossing iron bars about always did make me thirsty,' he said, 'especially when they were white hot. Come on, Loki, it's time we were going home. I'm afraid it turned out to be a working holiday after all.'

The stealing of Thor's hammer

The god Thor always resented the disdainful way he had been treated by King Loki of Outgard. He was quite determined that one day he would get his own back. Then a dreadful thing happened which made him fear that revenge might prove impossible: his hammer was stolen!

One evening he had retired as usual after a hearty supper in his palace of Bilskirnir and in an unusually tidy mood he placed his shoes together neatly, folded his clothes and laid his hammer on the table next to his pillow before getting into bed beside Sif.

Daylight was squeezing through the gaps in the shutters and the dawn chorus of birdsong was pealing in from the country-side when Thor awoke from a disturbing dream. He fancied in his sleep that a thief had crept into the bedroom and had stolen the one sure protection the gods had against the giants – his hammer. Half awake, he fumbled a hand out of the sheets and felt along the top of the bedside table. It was empty.

He sat up in bed with such a jolt that his wife Sif was shot out onto the floor. Before she could open her mouth to protest, Thor was yelling, 'My hammer! My hammer's been stolen! Æsir! Elves! Quick! Wait! No! Yes! Who's stolen my hammer? LOKI! LOKEE . . .!' and his red hair and beard tossed about in all directions as he wrathfully dragged on his clothes. He absent-mindedly picked the aggrieved Sif off the floor and put her back into bed, by which time Loki had come running up panting.

'You had anything to do with this, Loki?' bellowed Thor.
'What, what . . .?' gasped Loki as Thor gripped him by the scruff.
'My hammer – have you stolen it?'
'No, no, no,' stammered Loki. 'Only one lot dare do that, and you don't need me to tell you who they are. The giants!'
'Come on then!' cried Thor, 'My chariot – you are coming with me to Jotunheim to get it back!' and he started to drag Loki downstairs to the stables.
'Stop!' shouted Loki. 'Do have the sense to stop! Can't you see that's just what the giants want? Without your hammer

you'd be killed. We need stealth here. We need guile.'

'Well, you're the one for that,' replied Thor, simmering down, 'What do you suggest?'

The upshot was that Loki volunteered to borrow Freya's feather coat and fly as a hawk into Jotunheim to find out if possible what had happened to Thor's hammer. He winged his way swiftly over the ocean to the shores of Jotunheim and across the tops of the towering forest trees towards the mountains and the stronghold of King Loki.

From a distance he saw the king sitting on the gravemound of his ancestors just outside the city walls. There was a rune-carved stone commemorating the dead giants who were sitting upright in their high seats below in the mound waiting for the Ragnarok. Loki flew to the top of the tall stone and perched there. King Loki of Outgard was amusing himself plaiting gold leashes for his hunting dogs and trimming the manes of his horses. He glanced up.

'It's Loki, isn't it?' he asked.

'Yes,' replied the hawk, 'you are quite right, of course.'

'How goes it with the Æsir, and how with the elves? Very well, I trust?'

'The elves are upset and the Æsir worse. Someone has stolen Thor's hammer.'

'And who's the culprit?' asked King Loki of Outgard.

'You are, your gigantic majesty,' answered the Mischief Maker at which the giant let out such an exploding guffaw of cruel laughter that his horses shied in fear and his hounds cringed in terror.

'There's no use pretending with a clever fellow like you,' he said. 'You are quite right. I *have* stolen Thor's hammer; and the Thundering Nuisance will only get it back on conditions.'

'What conditions?'

'Don't think the hammer can be regained by force. It can't. I have buried it deep in the earth, seven leagues down. Only one thing will redeem it. You must bring me the goddess Freya to be my wife!'

Loki made no reply but flew straight back to Asgard and before he could alight Thor was asking him for news.

'Tell me at once, before you perch,' he cried, 'have you found out where my hammer is?'

The Mischief Maker explained precisely all he knew and told the terms necessary for retrieving the hammer. He had scarcely taken off the feather coat when Thor was dragging him to Freya's palace, bursting into it without any politeness or ceremony.

'Here's your feather coat, dear Freya,' said Thor, 'thanks for the loan of it. Now hurry up please and find yourself a bride's veil.'

'A bride's veil?' asked Freya, surprised. 'Who's getting married?'

'You are,' said Thor.

'I?' exclaimed Freya beginning to get angry, 'to whom, pray? Or is it a secret?'

'It's no secret,' said the simple Thor, 'to Loki of Outgard, of course.'

Freya's lovely breasts rose with such fury that her famous necklace Brisingamen snapped apart and the precious jewels scattered across the marble floor. She picked up the nearest weapon to hand, a distaff, and started to belabour Loki, shouting, 'I shan't, I shan't, I shan't!' It was no use trying to reason with her. She flatly refused to marry any giant even though he was a king.

Such a serious situation had to be made known to Odin. At once, he called a council meeting of all the Æsir and without delay they sat in deliberation upon their judgement stools. 'Who's first with any ideas?' asked Odin.

Tyr suggested an armed invasion of Jotunheim. Niord agreed, saying it should be an attack by sea and land and air with the Valkyries on their flying horses spear-heading the aerial battalions.

Loki said, 'I can tell you this: a direct attack will be useless. Let me remind you of the magic spells employed by the giant king to frustrate Thor in the past. Even if an attack was successful, the hammer would still lie hidden. There is only one way to get it back and that is to trick King Loki of Outgard into producing it.'

Heimdall, the whitest and sometimes the wisest of the gods said he had an idea.

'If we were to dress Thor himself up as a bride and send Loki disguised as a handmaid to do the talking, then once the hammer is brought out Thor can snatch it up and – hey presto! – heads will roll!'

'Jumping Jormungander!' shouted Thor, foaming at the mouth. 'Vexatious Vergelmir! Nobody dresses me up as a woman!'

But it was no use Thor's continuing to protest. Heimdall's suggestion was voted best in the end and the Thunderer had to submit to being clothed in petticoats to hide his hairy legs and a long-sleeved blouse stuffed out a bit in the appropriate places, topped by an embroidered tunic. Brooches were pinned onto his false bust and a set of housewife's keys was set to dangle from his girdle. To show he really was 'Freya', he had to wear the goddess's famous necklace, now repaired, Brisingamen. And to complete the disguise he was draped to the waist in a white bride's veil. Loki in turn was dressed up as a woman, a rather saucy lady's maid.

Thor's goats were led from the stable and harnessed to the chariot.

'Come on there, Toothgnasher! Gee up, Toothgrinder!' he shouted and cracked his whip while the smile vanished from Loki's lips as he nearly slipped out of the back. In a flash of lightning they were halfway across the sky.

In Jotunheim King Loki of Outgard heard the thunder of the chariot wheels and he called out to his servants to strew the carved wooden settles with cushions and goat skins to make them comfortable, to broach the sparkling, foamy ale, to set up the trestle tables and prepare the wedding feast for him and his new bride the lovely, the delectable, the incomparable Freya. He rubbed his gigantic hands with satisfaction as he thought of all his possessions, of the gold-horned oxen with jet black hides thronging his paddocks, of his horses and hounds, his hunting hawks, of the gold and jewels in his iron-bound coffers; he seemed to need only one thing to complete his happiness – the goddess Freya.

By the time the 'bride' and her 'lady's maid' had arrived it was early evening and the banquet was ready.

The bride was placed on King Loki's right hand and the maid on his left. The giant was very surprised when, during the feasting, the bride had no difficulty in despatching a whole ox, eight fine salmon and all the dainties intended for the lady giants. He was even more astonished to see this mountain of food washed down with three firkins of mead – and a firkin holds nine gallons!

'I don't think I ever saw a giant maiden with such a thirst or such an appetite,' he said.

'It *is* unusual,' said the cunning lady's maid, 'but you have to remember that when Freya knew she was going to marry you . . .' and here Loki was forced to gulp as he thought of the thumping lie he was about to tell, 'she was so excited, your majesty, that she couldn't eat for a week. Not a morsel passed her lovely lips. When we arrived here she was ravenous.'

'You can say that again,' muttered King Loki. He was getting impatient and wanted to steal a kiss from the bride so he lifted a corner of her veil.

Loki was petrified. And the giant king's hair almost stood on end at the sight of the flashing eyes he saw there in the lacy shadows. Handmaid Loki hastened to tell him not to worry, Freya's eyes were rather red because she had not been able to sleep for a week before coming to Outgard.

At last King Loki of Outgard called for the marriage to be solemnized in the traditional way by the bride and groom swearing their vows on Thor's hammer. The hammer was fetched from its hiding-place and laid on the bride's lap while the happy pair placed their hands on it and swore to be true to each other.

Thor's hand was underneath and when he felt Mullicrusher within his grasp once more all his confidence returned. He did not bother to throw off his veil. With one great lunge he felled his old enemy the giant king.

Then the pair of imposters strode out of the hall, mounted the chariot and rattled jubilantly back to Asgard again.

The death of Balder

The three mysterious beings who had spent so long talking to King Gylfi now assumed a very grave demeanour and High said: 'It is time to tell you of events which to the gods seem most ominous. As big things grow from little, so the start of this disaster was small of itself, simply this: Balder the Good had a bad dream.'

It appeared that Balder had dreamed a dream in which his life was threatened. How or why, he could not say, but he told the Æsir of his uneasiness and Odin thought the portents so serious that he decided to act himself. He went alone to High Nest and sat on the throne which allowed him to see over all the nine worlds. A swirl of mist and snowflakes formed in his mind's eye and he sensed that he was seeing a remote and desolate corner of Niflheim. Through the fog he glimpsed a long hump-back of snow-covered earth over a grave. He knew it to be the ancient burial place of Volva the Seeress. He realized then that he had to consult her ghost.

Secretly, very early one morning, Odin threw a saddle over Sleipnir's back, led him from Valhalla stables and rode down the skies. He galloped his steed as far as the confines of Hel, dropping down, ever down into darkness and cold. At last he came to the sheer black precipice wall of Gnipahellir and the mouth of Hel where, in the darkness, like a monstrous dog in a kennel, bayed and growled the blood-flecked Garmr. When the hound recognized the Father of All and his eight-legged horse, he whined and slunk into a corner, and Odin passed by. Odin had no intention of letting the Queen of Hel know of his intrusion into her territories; but as he stole through the eerie and mysterious realm of Niflheim, thronged with ghosts, he saw from far off a great deal of activity going on inside her palace. It seemed to him that preparations were afoot for the reception of an important guest.

Odin walked Sleipnir to the eastern wall of Hel's vast estates where the grave he was seeking lay. He stood moodily looking at the ground in the silence of impending doom; he saw the grave mound come and go beneath the swirling mist. He concentrated all his divine power and uttering spells and magic runes he called upon the occupant of the grave to rise and speak to him.

The mist thinned and through it he saw a head, or the apparition of a head, with long grey elf-locked hair and a face so ancient that the skull gleamed through beneath. It was Volva the Seeress. She could see not only backwards into the black hole of forgotten time, but forward too until there was nothing left to happen. Reluctantly, in a voice which seemed a rustle of long lost ages past, Volva whispered, 'What man is this, to me unknown, who draws me from my dying grave? Countless ages was I drifted with snow; I was drenched with rain; I was dank with dew; too long have I been dead.'

'I am Rover son of Battler,' said Odin. 'I come from above and wish to know for whom the benches in Hel's abode are strewn with cushions and the tables laid for eating and drinking?'

The seeress answered, 'Your runes are powerful, Rover son of Battler, now know this: the ale is brewed and the mead sparkles bright for Balder, Odin's son. Hel will rejoice at his coming, though the Æsir mourn. Unwilling I speak; now let me sink back to rest.'

'Stay Volva! Wait! My questions are not yet done. Tell me, I conjure thee, who will be the slayer of Balder, who will murder Odin's son?'

'The blind god Hoder's hand will carry the fateful branch. Unwillingly I have spoken; now I would be quiet.'

Odin cried, 'Wait Volva, wait! Sink not yet! Tell me first who will avenge Balder's death?'

Volva answered, 'Rinda the maiden bears Vali to Odin in the Caverns of the West. This wondrous child shall neither wash his hands nor comb his lustrous hair until he has brought Balder's slayer to the funeral pyre. Unwillingly I have spoken, now let me sink to rest.'

'No, Volva, no! By the magic runes I command thee! Answer this last question: what is the word that Odin will whisper into the ear of his dead son Balder as he lies on the funeral pyre?'

The lipless mouth of Volva opened black. She shrieked and pointed at Odin with a bony finger: 'You are not Rover son of Battler! Only Odin knows that he will give a message to the dead Balder and only Odin knows what that message will be! You are Odin! Odin! Odin!'

Sadly, Odin mounted Sleipnir and galloped back to Asgard. He summoned all the Æsir to meet in council. He did not tell of his journey down to Hel, he only said that Balder's life was threatened and that moves must be made to protect him. After long deliberations all the gods and goddesses agreed that a suggestion put forward by Frigg should be acted upon. Frigg suggested simply that she, as Mother of All, should exact promises from fire and water, iron and every sort of metal, stones, earth, trees, diseases, beasts, birds, poisons and serpents that they would never harm Balder. It was no sooner agreed than it was done. Everybody and everything loved Balder the Good so much that they gave their promise at once never to injure him.

A surprising outcome of the oaths was that Balder never cut himself with a knife, never grazed his skin on rock or stone, never pricked himself with a pin, never stubbed his toe, never bumped his head. When his brothers realized this, they made it a sport and pastime at their meetings and parties to get him to stand up while everyone who felt like it either shot arrows at him or cut and thrust with swords and spears or merely threw stones. No matter what weapons were used against him, he never took the slightest harm.

Only Loki the Mischief Maker did not like it one little bit. His dearest wish was to see Balder hurt or even killed and he puzzled over how he could hurt the god that nothing would harm.

Society in those days was rather free and easy, even in Asgard, and people offered a night's lodging to complete strangers who happened to be on the road or at least gave

them a meal in return for news. One morning
an old crone swathed in shawls wandered
up to the kitchen door of Frigg's palace
Fensalir. Her nose was long and warty and her
baggy eyes dropped rheum. She was given
food and drink, and she asked to be allowed
to pass the time of day with the mistress
of the house. When she was shown into the
cloudy hall, Frigg, to make conversation,
enquired if the old woman had walked by the
gods' meeting place that day and did she
notice what they were doing?

'Trying to kill Balder, it seemed to me,' carped
the crone.

Frigg smiled gently, 'Oh they'll never do
that!' she said.

'But I saw them with me own eyes a-throwing
spears an' shooting arrows at him,' piped
the ugly old woman, 'and he without a stitch
of armour.'

Frigg explained patiently, 'Neither weapon
nor wand will ever wound or even hurt
my dear Balder. I have their given word – all
of them.'

The old crone croaked, 'Do you mean to
say, my lady, that every single thing has sworn
to protect Balder from harm?'

'As a matter of honest fact,' Frigg said, 'there
is one young sprout which is too weak
to grow on its own and has to have an oak
tree to support it – it's called Mistletoe and it
grows in a wood behind Valhalla – I couldn't
ask *that* for its promise because it is far too
immature to swear oaths.'

The old crone, who was in fact Loki in
disguise, turned on 'her' heel without as
much as a thank-you for the refreshment, and
lost no time in finding the mistletoe and
cutting it down. It was not difficult to spot,
even in the gloomy forest, with its light green
leaves and pretty pearl-like fruit. Loki
took a spear and fastened a sharp mistletoe
point in place of the iron blade. He walked to
the gods' meeting place where they were
still amusing themselves hurling anything they
could lay their hands on at Balder. On the
edge of the ring of gods stood a disconsolate
figure, the blind god Hoder. He could hear
his brothers laughing and shouting and

enjoying themselves, and he felt left out. A
leery voice whispered in his ear,
'Why aren't you shooting at Balder?'

Hoder started and said, 'Because I can't see
where he is; and another thing – I have
nothing to throw. The Æsir don't like me to
have swords and things; they think I might
hurt myself.'

Then Loki said, 'Do as the others are doing
and show honour to Balder as they do.
I'll guide you to where he's standing. Here,
pitch this shaft at him!'

Hoder grasped the mistletoe-tipped spear
and just as Loki had told him, threw it at
Balder. The shaft flew full at his heart and he
fell down dead to the ground.

As soon as they realized that Balder had
been killed, the gods were struck dumb. They
looked at one another with just a single
thought in their heads: 'Who did this shameful
thing? And how?'

Odin's sorrow was more bitter than that of
the other gods, although the actual event

gods' vessels and the funeral pyre for Balder's body was built on its deck.

Then Balder's body was carried shoulder high onto the ship, and when his wife, Nanna saw it she cried aloud in her grief and anguish; for she would not allow Balder to sail away alone and she perished with his body in the fire. At the very last minute they hoisted the sail. Thor then stepped to the front and blessed the funeral pyre with Mulli-crusher. As he did so a dwarf named Lit ran in under his feet; Thor lunged at him savagely with his toe, flinging him into the midst of the blaze and he burned to death.

All kinds of people gathered for the burning. The mourners were led by Odin and Frigg and the Valkyries were there also and the ravens. There stood Frey in his chariot drawn by his two boars Golden Bristles and Tearing Tusks; Heimdall riding his horse Gold-Topping; Freya with her cats; then thronged a great host of frost giants and hill trolls peeping in the background behind the family. Odin flung into the fire his gold ring Draupnir the Dropper. Balder's horse in full harness had already been put to death and laid on the pyre.

And so the blazing funeral ship, with full sail set, left Asgard's shore. Darkness was falling and the great vessel began to gather way like a monstrous swan breasting the flame-flecked waves. They had built the fire in front of the sail so that the wind would not blow the fiery tongues into the fabric and lick it away before the ship had been swept into the main sea. As the fire roared, the bulging sail glowed with the conflagration in front of it, and those on shore saw the black rod of the mast and the thin ratlins and backstay silhouetted before the amber light. Night came down. Soon the longship was raked from stem to stern with crackling fire until her planks were carbonized and her thicker ribs showed dark. Then, in the far distance she was lost. Either what was left sank hissing into the sea or else she dipped below the horizon and the spark winked out.

All this time Hermod was journeying

came as no surprise to him. He knew what the slaying of Balder meant: it was the beginning of the End.

When the Æsir had composed themselves a little, Frigg spoke up.
'Who is there,' she asked, 'on our side who will earn the love and undying gratitude of all the gods by riding down the road to Hel and trying to find the ghost of Balder? Who will ask the ransom Queen Hel desires – providing she is willing to allow Balder to come back home to Asgard?'

The one known as Hermod the Swift, a son of Odin and Frigg, said he was ready to go on the dangerous mission.

Then Odin's horse Sleipnir was led from the stables; Hermod quietly said 'good-bye', jumped into the saddle and galloped away.

The gods gently lifted up Balder's corpse and carried it down to the sea shore. Balder's longship was there. Because of its beautiful carvings of interlacing rings it was called Ringhorni. It was one of the greatest of the

towards Hel. He rode nine days and nights down ravines ever darker and deeper, meeting no-one until he came to the banks of the river Gioll. He followed this as far as the Gioll bridge, a bridge roofed with burning gold. The name of the maiden who stands guard at the bridge is Modgud. 'Who are you that makes my bridge sound so,' she asked him. 'Yesterday five droves of dead men passed this way, but the bridge echoed less than under you alone. And you have not the pallor of a dead man. Why then are you riding down the Hel Way?' Hermod replied, 'I ride to Hel to seek out Balder. You don't happen to have set eyes on Balder on the road to Hel?'

She said Balder had already ridden over Gioll Bridge 'and the road to Hel lies downward still and to the north.'

Hermod galloped on until he came to Hel's barred gate, where he stepped down from Sleipnir's back and tightened the girths. He mounted again and raked his spurs along the animal's ribs. The stallion sprang so high that there was plenty of twilight between him and the bars. And Hermod rode on to the hall of Hel where he dismounted again and went inside. There were his brother Balder and his sister-in-law Nanna sitting on thrones. He was invited to eat and drink, and he stayed with Balder for that night.

Next morning Hermod begged Queen Hel to let Balder ride back home with him to resume the happy life they had all formerly led in Asgard. He explained how greatly the gods were grieving. But the Queen of Death turned her livid side towards him and appeared unmoved. Hermod shivered at the sight but continued to plead. Always he returned to the same theme, that because of Balder's death everything in heaven and earth was heartbroken. At last Hel turned her normal side to him and seemed to soften. She said:

'It can soon be proved whether Balder was as greatly loved as you say. Tell Frigg I will make a bargain with her. If every single creature up above, dead or alive, really is mourning for Balder and is willing to shed tears to prove it, then he shall be restored to the gods. If but one single thing speaks out against him or refuses to mourn, then Hel holds what she has!'

Hermod stood up and Balder saw him outside. Balder pulled the ring Draupnir off his wrist and sent it back to Odin as a keepsake, while his wife Nanna sent some linen and other gifts to Frigg, and to her dear friend, a goddess named Fulla, a gold finger ring.

Wasting no more time, Hermod rode back to Asgard and related all his news, everything he had seen and everything he had heard.

Immediately, the Æsir sent messengers to all corners of the Upperworld asking for Balder to be wept un-dead. And everything was willing to weep, gods, men, beasts, earth, stones, trees and every metal – even to this day metals have not forgotten how to shed tears when they are brought out of the frost into the warmth. At last the messengers returned to Valhalla. One of them happened to be passing a cave where he noticed an old witch crouching. 'Nearly missed this one,' he thought to himself, 'I'd better get her to weep.' He went inside the cavern. 'We're asking people to cry for Balder,' he said. The old woman appeared to be deaf. 'We want you to shed a few tears for Balder!' he shouted.

The witch looked up with baleful eyes, hard and dry as pebbles. 'What's your name?' shouted the messenger. 'My name is Dry-Eyes!' she cackled, 'and if you think I'll weep for Balder you are greatly mistaken. Living or dead I never loved him! Let Hel hold what she has!' and she hooted with horrible laughter.

Of course, the gods were inconsolable when they heard of the witch's refusal. Because of her, Balder was doomed to remain in the Underworld. They grieved at the wickedness of the creature and wondered whoever she could be. Then they saw the truth: only Loki the Mischief Maker could be so evil – he was the witch Dry-Eyes. In their furious anger they determined to put him away for ever.

The gods' revenge

Loki was well aware that the gods, in their grief and anger at his terrible act of murder, would think of a most fearful punishment to fit the enormity of his crime. So he vanished away at once and hid.

Though he was cunning, even his best efforts were useless against the might of Odin. The father of the gods sat on his throne High Nest and saw where Loki had built himself a house on a distant mountain. The house had windows and doors on all four sides so that he could both see anyone approach and escape before he was surrounded. During the daytime he changed into the shape of a salmon, haunting a pool below a nearby waterfall called Glittering Force.

In the evenings Loki passed his time inventing something he had first thought of when he borrowed Ran's magnic net to catch the dwarf Andvari. From linen thread knotted into a squared web he made what has come to be known as a fishing net. With this he caught his food. But Loki's time was running out. Odin had told the Æsir where his hiding place was and a hunting party set off to trap him.

That particular evening, all unsuspecting, Loki was weaving his new invention for the next day's fishing when through one of the four windows he became aware of the gods' approach. He had been sitting in front of the fire and the logs were burning low. In an instant he flung the net into the embers and darted out of the door farthest from his pursuers.

The gods burst into his house, led by Kvasir who was known especially for his wisdom. Kvasir saw at once that the house was empty but he noticed that the fire was webbed with white ash where the net had burned.
'Loki has been catching fish,' he said, turning to the other gods. He saw a few silver salmon scales glittering on the chair.
'In fact I should think Loki may be concealing himself in the form of a fish.'

At once the gods began to make a fishing net for themselves, following the pattern of the ashes of Loki's burnt one. They believed they would find him lurking in the pool below the fall.

Next morning they all went to the pool into which Glittering Force plunged with a noise like thunder. Thor, standing on one bank, gripped one end of the net while the rest of the gods hauled on the other from the far side of the pool.

Under the clear water of the pool, Loki could see the net closing in behind him. He flashed in front of it and hung still at the bottom between two stones. The lower cord of the net passed over his silver back. He breathed out with relief and Kvasir saw a string of bubbles come to the surface. 'We've missed him!' he shouted, 'Pull the net back towards the pool!'

'Wait!' cried Thor, 'Let me hang stones in the lower part of the net so that he can't swim underneath!'

Loki swam in front of the net but when he saw the pool was becoming too shallow for him, he twisted about and twirled his fish tail so vigorously that he shot up through the water and dived into the air. He passed clean over the top cord of the net and raced towards the plunging cataract.

The gods let out shouts of surprise and anger and once more altered direction with their net. Loki began to leap up the rushing falls. Frey saw that he was going to get away and ran round the bank to station himself at the top of the waterfall.

Once again salmon-Loki turned back towards the pool but this time Thor had waded out into the middle of the water. As the net approached him, Loki leaped again.

Thor was waiting with both hands open, his fingers stuck out like the prongs of two rakes. That is what they looked like to the terrified Loki. He tried to wriggle his slippery body aside and over the backs of Thor's hands but the god grabbed after him and held him. His silver scales were so wet and shiny that Thor let him slip through his fingers as far as the fish's tail. There he clutched hard with a crushing grip. 'You'd better change your shape to the evil one we know,' growled Thor, 'or I'll hold you here out of the water until you choke.'

Loki transformed himself to his old familiar shape only to find himself held upside down by the heels. Thor allowed his head to drop below the surface of the pool and Loki choked and spluttered. Thor would have finished him off then and there but the other gods cried, 'No! No! Death is too good for him! Drag him to the Underworld and shackle him there for ever!'

Thor also knew that it was Odin's decree that Loki should be bound in the Underworld, so they dragged him off to a dark and dismal hole not far from the place where they had tethered the wolf Fenrir.

Thor prised three rocks out of the cavern floor and set them up on edge. He split a V-shape out of the top of the three rocks.

It was obvious that only a magic bond would hold Loki's limbs fast and Odin knew what it must be. He ordered Loki's two sons Vali and Nari to be captured. The gods charmed Vali into the shape of a wolf and he immediately set upon his brother Nari and savaged him to death. The gods took Nari's entrails and used them to bind Loki so that he lay prone along the three rocks standing on edge: one stuck under his shoulders, the second under his loins and the third under the hollow of his knees. The magic entrails held fast his wrists, knees and ankles and they bolted him to the rocks with iron. Finally, Skadi the giantess, daughter of Thiazzi and now Niord's wife, caught a poisonous snake and trapped it by the tail so that it wriggled above Loki's head, dripping its venom into his open face. When the poison ran into his eyes, he was thrown into such terrific convulsions that all Midgard shook.

Loki's wife Sigyn was still faithful to him. 'I will sit with him for ever,' she said, 'if you will only let me hold a basin under the poison drops.'

So Sigyn sits patiently beside her husband in the dark, slimy cave. When her basin is full to overflowing she hurries away to pour out the venom. In the meantime the snake's fangs still drip poison onto Loki's face and Midgard is once again shaken by earthquakes.

And there lies Loki fast bound until the Ragnarok.

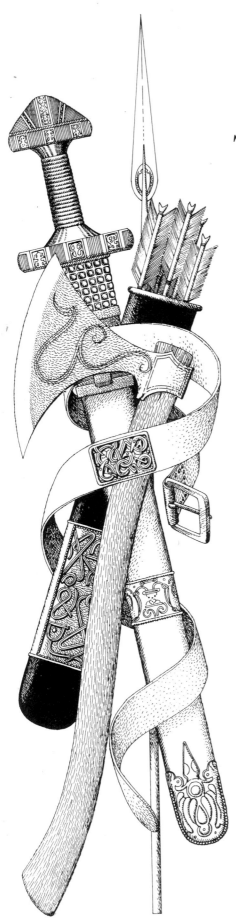

The Ragnarok, doom of the god

If the three mysterious beings looked grave before they spoke of the death of Balder, their sadness when they began to speak of the Ragnarok was beyond description.

King Gylfi pulled his cloak around him. 'Ragnarok,' he said, 'it is a curious word, one which has always struck terror. What exactly does it mean?'

'It means,' said High, 'nothing more nor less than the doom of the divine powers. And that can only mean the end of all who are dependent on the gods, the end of everything.'

Gylfi shivered. 'Is Ragnarok really the end?' he asked.

'We shall see,' said High.

The details of Ragnarok are many and terrible. When that dread catastrophe approaches, the first to notice any change in the established order of things will be men on Midgard, those descendants of Ash and Elm created so many aeons ago by Odin and his brothers. How will they know that Ragnarok is coming? First, they will experience a world-wide war. On Midgard there will follow one after the other three terrible years during which the whole world will be plunged into battle and strife. Sordid greed and envy will drive men to acts of madness and make them kill each other indiscriminately, brother murdering brother, father slaying son and son father, none showing mercy in unnatural crimes and murders.

Immediately following that cruel war will come the Fimbul winter, the monstrous winter which is really three winters rolled into one with no summer in between. At that time, blizzards will drive mercilessly from every point of the compass at once, frost will be hard as iron and winds sharp as knives.

Nor will the heavens offer any comfort, no matter how men look to them, because something that seems to human beings an unimaginable disaster will occur: the wolf will swallow the sun! At one bite, the other wolf will gorge the moon, while all the stars will fall down from their places in the darkened sky.

The next sign will be that the ground will tremble and shake, forests will be torn up by the roots, crags crack from top to bottom and all fetters and bonds will be smashed and split. The elves and the dwarfs will crouch shivering by their shattered rock-holes, moaning in bewilderment at this upheaval which they cannot understand.

As the earth's crust splits and shakes, the wolf Fenrir, shackled by the gods in the Underworld, will break loose! The heaving land will be flooded by a tidal wave of waters caused by the World Serpent when, in a gigantic fury, he frees his tail from his jaws and buckles up out of the sea!

Then the dead men's nail ship Naglfar will crowd on her crew and slip her moorings at Corpse Strand where she has waited from time out of mind for this moment. At the helmsman's cry her myriad oars will plunge together into the great waves raised by the Serpent, and the waves will carry her not only over Midgard but up to the shores of Asgard itself. Her crew are all the Undead from Hel and her captain and steersman is the cruellest enemy gods and men ever had: Loki. He will break free from his fetters at the first earthquake, joining forces with his terrible sons Fenrir the wolf and the serpent Jormungander. Fenrir will lope along with his mighty jaws wide open, his lower teeth raking the earth, his upper scraping heaven, while flames gush from his mouth and nostrils. The World Serpent will blow in front of him rolling clouds of poisonous fumes which will envelop both earth and sky in smoke and stench.

At the height of the tumult and noise, the sky will split apart and through the rift will gallop the blazing cavalry of the fire giants from Muspellheim. Surt, who has stood since the beginning in the furnace, will spearhead the charge on a fiery horse, splashing flames in front and behind, thrusting before him in his outstretched arm the sword whose burning blade is brighter than a thousand suns. The hooves of the stallions of the fire giants will be all on fire as they pound up over the bridge of Bifrost. The many-coloured rainbow will break and crumble behind them.

All the hosts of Muspell will move steadily on in massed array, making for the battlefield on the vast plain known as Vigrith.

Fenrir the wolf and the World Serpent will be there. There too will march the men from Hel, disembarked from Naglfar and led by Loki. Shoulder to shoulder with them will tramp the mountain and frost giants, marshalled by their own monstrous generals. The battlefield Vigrith stretches a hundred leagues in every direction, but the ranks of the forces of evil will fill it from one end to the other as they wait in fearsome array to fight the gods.

On the morning of Ragnarok the cockerel Gullinkambi will crow his first and last 'cock-a-doodle-do' from his perch on Valhalla roof, startling out of their sleep the champions in the hall below. At the same moment Heimdall's keen eyes and ears will catch the first tiny rustle of the earthquake and the quiver of moving rocks. He will stand out on the walls of his palace by Bifrost bridge and raise Giallarhorn to his lips, drawing into his lungs a full, hissing breath. His trumpet will crackle out such a startling clarion call to arms that all the gods and their helpers will stand to at once, excited, the blood roaring through their veins. The blast from Heimdall's bugle will re-echo from every nook and cranny of the nine worlds in the Tree. At its ominous sound the Tree itself will start to tremble and then to shake: every corner of the universe will be seized with terror.

Then Odin will leap onto Sleipnir's back and thunder like the storm wind all the way to Mimir's well to ask advice from Mimir's head. It will be in vain, for this time the head will not answer. Odin will gallop back to Asgard with a heavy heart for he must lead his forces, knowing that nothing can now prevent the end of everything.

With Heimdall's bugle call to arms still resounding in their ears, the Æsir and the Einheriar, the champions of Valhalla, will buckle on their armour, seize their weapons and shields and ride in ranks to their battle stations. Odin, wearing his golden helmet and sparkling war-coat, carrying his spear Gungnir, will canter out in front to lead them. Thor's chariot will rumble at his right